JOURNAL

OF THE

UNITED STATES ASSOCIATION

OF

CHARCOAL IRON WORKERS.

Index to Volumes 1 and 2, April, 1880, to December, 1881, inclusive.

A.

B.

C.

D.

E.

F.

G.

H.

I.

K.

L.

M.

N.

O.

P.

Q.

R.

S.

T.

U.

V.

W.

JOURNAL

OF

UNITED STATES ASSOCIATION

OF

CHARCOAL IRON WORKERS.

EDITED BY THE SECRETARY.

No. 1. APRIL, 1880.

Minutes of the Meetings.

On June 18, 1879, a circular was issued by Messrs. Valentine, Fuller, and Wiestling of Pennsylvania, and William Milnes, Jr., of Virginia, inviting all producers of charcoal iron to meet for for mutual acquaintance. In response to which a meeting was held at the Continental hotel, in Philadelphia, on July 10, 1879.

At eleven, A. M., the meeting was called to order by Colonel George B. Wiestling, who nominated Robert Valentine, of Bellefonte, Pennsylvania, as chairman, and C. E. Coffin, of Muirkirk, Maryland, as secretary. The motion was unanimously carried.

After brief remarks the chair announced the meeting open for business.

Upon motion of Mr. A. G. Curtin, Jr., a committee of three (Messrs. Curtin, Townsend, and McCoy) were appointed to invite Mr. James M. Swank, secretary of the American Iron and Steel Association, to participate in the proceedings. Owing to the absence of Mr. Swank, he was represented by Mr. G. W. Cope.

Mr. J. C. Fuller offered the following:

Resolved, That a committee be appointed by the president, to draft a consitution and set of by-laws for the organization of the National Association of Charcoal Iron Manufacturers; to report at a meeting to be held on Thursday, the 18th of September, 1879, at ten o'clock, A. M., in Parlor "C," Continental hotel, Philadelphia.

Resolved, That to the same committee be referred the nomination of officers for the permanent organization.

Resolved, That the present officers of this meeting hold over until the organization of the association is effected, and their successors are elected, and that we be subject to their call for an earlier meeting if a necessity arises for the same in their judgments.

Resolved, That notices be sent to every charcoal iron manufacturer in the United States, inviting them to attend the meeting, and to coöperate with us.

The resolutions were adopted, and the chair appointed as the committee Messrs. Fuller, Wiestling, Townsend, and Coffin.

On motion the chairman was added to the committee.

After an interchange of views, the meeting adjourned until September 18, unless sooner called by the chairman.

Attest: C. E. COFFIN,
Secretary pro tem.

CONTINENTAL HOTEL,
PHILADELPHIA, *September* 18, 1879.

In reponse to the invitation issued, the meeting of charcoal iron producers was called to order at ten, A. M., Mr. Robert Valentine, president *pro tem.*, in the chair.

The committee appointed at the meeting on July 10, to draft constitution and nominate officers, presented their report.

The constitution as read was considered, and after some amendments, was adopted, as follows: (See page 4.)

The meeting then proceeded to the election of officers, which resulted in selecting the following gentlemen:

President.

Colonel GEORGE B. WIESTLING, Superintendent Mont Alto Iron Company, Pennsylvania.

Vice President.

Hon. WILLARD WARNER, President Tecumseh Iron Company, Alabama.

Board of Managers.

ALFRED L. TYLER, President Woodstock Iron Company, Alabama.

ROBERT VALENTINE, Bellefonte Iron Works, Pennsylvania.

J. C. FULLER, President South Mountain Mining and Iron Company, Pennsylvania.

HENRY T. TOWNSEND, Treasurer Logan Iron and Steel Company, Pennsylvania.

A. G. CURTIN, Jr., Eagle Iron Works, Pennsylvania.

CHARLES E. COFFIN, President Muirkirk Iron Company, Maryland.

CHARLES CAMPBELL, Secretary Hecla Iron and Mining Company, Ohio.

J. C. GARRET, Tennessee.

M. S. EIFURT, Kentucky.

S. A. JOHNSON, New York.

(Additional managers for States now represented will be elected at the next meeting.)

After the election of officers, the meeting adjourned until five P. M.

Upon re-convening, the secretary read a paper upon the charcoal iron industry of the United States,* prepared by John Birkinbine, general manager of the South Mountain Mining and Iron Company, for which a vote of thanks was unanimously given.

Mr. J. Antoine Mathieu addressed the meeting upon the importance and economy of utilizing the acetic vapors generated in carbonizing wood.

On motion, Hon. D. J. Morrell, president, and James M. Swank, secretary of the American Iron and Steel Association were elected honorary members.

---

* As the features of this paper will be treated of in the statistics of the Charcoal Iron Works, now in preparation, its publication in the JOURNAL is unnecessary.

The gentlemen present then paid dues for the various works which they represented, and after general discussion and interchange of information, the meeting adjourned.

Attest: C. E. COFFIN,
Secretary pro tem.

Constitution of the United States Association of Charcoal Iron Workers.

ARTICLE I.—*Preamble.*

The objects of this association are to procure regularly, statistics of all manufacturers of iron by the use of charcoal as fuel; to provide for the mutual interchange of practical and scientific knowledge and experience in this branch of metallurgy, and to take proper measures for advancing and protecting the interests of the trade in all its branches.

ARTICLE II.—*Name.*

The organization shall be known as the "United States Association of Charcoal Iron Workers."

ARTICLE III.—*Management.*

The affairs of the association shall be conducted by a president, vice president, and a board of managers, elected annually. The board of managers shall consist of one manager for every five members for each State represented in the association, provided that each State represented shall be entitled to one manager.

An executive committee of three members shall be annually elected by the board of managers, and the president and vice president shall be *ex-officio* members of said committee.

ARTICLE IV.—*Finances.*

The funds of the association shall be subject to the control and disposition of the executive committee, who shall have power to select a secretary and treasurer, and fix compensation therefor; but the executive committee shall at no time enter into any debt or contract on behalf of the association, involving any liability on the part of the association, beyond the funds which may be in the treasury.

ARTICLE V.—*Membership.*

Any person practically engaged, or interested by reason of capital invested, in any process of charcoal iron production, may become a member of the association by paying an annual fee of five dollars, ($5 00:) *Provided,* That each iron works represented shall pay not less than ten dollars ($10 00) per annum into the treasury of the association as fees. All fees to be due when the membership is applied for, and thereafter on the first day of October in each year, being in advance.

ARTICLE VI.—*Rights and Penalties of Membership.*

Each member shall be entitled, either in person or by proxy, to one vote, and to participate in all meetings of the association, but no member in arrears for one year shall be entitled to vote, and any member who neglects or refuses to pay his annual fee for two years may forfeit his right of membership.

The resignation of any member not in arrears may be accepted.

ARTICLE VII.—*Honorary and Corresponding Members.*

Honorary and corresponding members may be elected at regular meetings of the association, and they shall not be liable to pay any fee.

ARTICLE VIII.—*Meetings.*

The executive committee shall provide for an annual meeting, and for such regular and special meetings of the association as it may deem fit for the interests of the trade; and it shall, at the written request of one third of the membership of the board of managers, call special meetings.

ARTICLE IX.

The executive committee shall have power to make such by-laws as they consider expedient for the government of their meetings, and they shall present at each annual meeting a report of the business of the association for the preceding year, including a record of receipts and expenditures by the treasurer.

Salutatory.

We have no apology, (except for editorial imperfections,) and but little explanation to offer in making our bow to the Charcoal Iron Workers of the country. The JOURNAL is the exponent of the association whose name it bears, and as such will be devoted to the advancement of the interests of the branch of metallurgy which the association represents.

That there is a field for such a publication we well know, and an honest effort will be made to occupy that field. The desire is to make the JOURNAL the authority on charcoal and charcoal iron. To do this the assistance of every one interested in the business is invoked. The various charcoal iron workers of the country have, in the aggregate, much valuable information, but it is so scattered that it is of little use even to the possessors. It is our desire, by collecting this data, to advance the general and individual interests to the trade, to improve and simplify processes, and publish information concerning the various special features of the business.

Papers on subjects of interests read at the association meetings, and the discussions upon them, will be published. Monographs on topics of particular importance to charcoal iron manufacturers will be incorporated. The operation of our various industrial works, and descriptions of districts, or of individual plants, will be a feature of the JOURNAL.

The technical publications will be examined, interesting items culled from them, and all possible means of obtaining information upon wood, charcoal, or charcoal iron will be employed.

The present number must not be considered as indicative of the standard which we purpose establishing for the JOURNAL; being the initial issue of the publication, the labor of its preparation became an individual one, and hence it cannot lay claim to the variety or ability which is expected to characterize future publications. If each one who reads its pages will contribute his mite of information, the JOURNAL will reach the highest expectations of its publishers. The papers have been prepared not as exhaustive treatises, but rather to invite discussion. The object has been to cover the ground generally so as to give to each branch of the trade some thing of possible value. It is our hope that by receiving the generous support of all the charcoal iron works, to be able to issue subsequent numbers at short intervals, and to add to their interest by illustrations explanatory of the subject matter of the text.

Although the subject of producing charcoal has received considerable attention from some scientists, their researches are either distributed through various publications as chapters, paragraphs, or sections, or else printed in foreign languages, so that there is practically no literature in the subject. The same may be said about charcoal irons, for, beyond sketches having a tendency more to the historical, than to either the practical or technical, but little has been published. It will be our object to give to the members of the Association, through the journal, a résumé of the information which has been published concerning the product we make, and the fuel we use. In short, we hope to make the journal the charcoal iron-workers' encyclopædia.

The quotations of market prices of charcoal irons is the result of personal correspondence with manufacturers throughout the country, and is given in this number as a matter of information and of record. While the United States Association of Charcoal Iron Workers does not attempt to make or control prices, it is the desire of the publishers to give data as to market prices in the JOURNAL for the information of the members, and as a reference for future use.

Charcoal Iron in Oregon.

Believing it will be a matter of general interest, we give place to a description of the Oswego Iron Company's blast furnace, the only one on the Pacific coast, situated at Oswego, Oregon, on the west side of the Willamette river, eight miles above Portland. It was built by the Oregon Iron Company, and went into blast August 22, 1867. From then until April 8, 1869, the furnace was in blast, producing twenty-three hundred and ninety-five tons of pig iron, an average of five and eighty-four one hundredths tons per day. The furnace was then blown out, and remained idle until March 13, 1874, when it was started up again; running to September 18, 1876, producing five thousand and seventy-five tons of pig iron, an average of eight and forty-five one hundredths tons per day.

During the time the Oregon Iron Company owned the property the furnace run ten hundred and thirteen days, producing seventy-four hundred and seventy tons of pig iron, or an average of seven and forty-four one hundredths tons per day.

The furnace was sold at sheriff's sale September 10, 1877, to satisfy a judgment in favor of its creditors, to the Oswego Iron Company, the present owners. S. H. Brown, president and treasurer, Portland; L. B. Seeley, agent, San Francisco; E. W. Crichton, secretary and superintendent, Oswego.

This company started the furnace June 10, 1878, running to to November 8, 1878, and produced eleven hundred and seventy tons of pig iron, an average of eight and sixty-two one hundredths tons per day. The height of the stack was then thirty-two feet; bosh, ten and a half feet. During the winter of 1878 and 1879 the furnace was remodeled, ten feet being added to the height of the stack, and the capacity of the hot blast increased. The size of the furnace is now—height, forty-two feet; bosh, nine feet six inches. The furnace went into blast April 23, 1879, and is still in. Up to January 1, 1880, it has produced in two hundred and six days, running time, twenty-three hundred tons of pig iron, an average of over eleven tons per day, and at the present time is turning out thirteen tons per day of No. 1 foundry hot-blast charcoal pig iron. The furnace was blown out March 26th, and the proprietors will remodel the inside of the furnace, and also will have a new double blowing engine, blast cylinders, five feet by four feet, set up, built by Smith Brothers & Watson, Portland; the object being to increase the capacity of the furnace to eighteen tons per day. The blowing machinery is driven by a thirty and a half feet water wheel, under forty feet head of water.

The company own over two thousand acres of land, having purchased the whole of the celebrated Prosser ore bed, located two and six tenths miles distant, and connect with furnace by a narrow guage railroad. The main entry to the mine extends into the hill over four hundred feet, showing on either side a solid front of over ten feet of iron ore. This ore is brown hematite, and averages in the furnace, raw, forty per cent. metallic iron. A letter just received from the superintendent states that it can be delivered in the ore shed at furnace for seventy-five cents per ton. The company had mined last year eight thousand tons iron ore, and had seven thousand cords of fir wood made into charcoal, and have now under contract for delivery this year twelve thousand tons iron ore and twelve thousand cords of wood to be made into charcoal in open pits, as they expect to make five thousand tons of pig iron this year.

A peculiarity of the work at the furnace is that all is done by single men, and the company own but one house.

The wood chopping is done by Chinamen.

The limestone comes from Washington Territory.

The company is represented in the association, and we publish this description as a sample of the value our journal may become to the members, scattered, as they are, so widely over the country, and as an item of especial interest on account of the furnace being the only one on the Pacific coast.

A charcoal furnace is projected by the Puget Sound Iron Company, to be located at Port Townsend, Washington Territory, about one hundred and eighty-five miles due north of the Oswego furnace.

Ourselves.

As the JOURNAL affords an opportunity to talk of and to each other not heretofore enjoyed, we may be pardoned for indulging in a little self glorification and mutual commisseration.

It is only those practically engaged in the business, who can appreciate the varied duties which the management of a charcoal iron works embraces.

The large iron and steel corporations of the country have their separate branches, each under charge of some one experinced in the specialty. The mining engineer attends to coal and ore mining. The blast furnace manager oversees the production of pig-iron. The mill superintendent supervises the manipulation of the iron in the heating and puddling furnaces, and through the rolls or hammers. The secretary, with assistants, keeps the books, and the treasurer pays the bills. The mechanical engineer attends to repairs and renewals, which are principally made in a well-appointed machine department. Sales agents dispose of the product of the works, and purchasing agents are often employed to buy supplies and material.

The chemist, by analytical research, guides the selection of ores and materials for the various purposes. The general manager must keep the individual departments up to their work, contend with transportation companies about freights, and attend the periodic dinners of the directory when a new departure is to be made, or dividends declared.

The extended business of these large industries make all the positions a necessity, and they are filled from the ablest specialists of the land. Few of the charcoal iron industries are of sufficient individual magnitude to permit of such a division of labor, and and if they were, their isolation and distance from the intellectual centers, in most cases, form barriers to encouraging experts to take up their abode in the mountains, unless compensation is made for the loss of the privileges of public libraries and technical society.

The manager of a charcoal iron works must, ordinarily, be boss wood chopper and collier, mining and mechanical engineer, blast furnace manager, forge superintendent, and be posted on horses, wagons, store accounts, buying and selling, book-keeping, and often represent the Government as post-master for sixty per cent. of the stamps he uses, with a few scattering added from the little community, of which he is the center. In fact, be Jack-of-all-trades.

He cannot follow the example of the manager who uses anthracite or coke for fuel, and order his supply by letter or through the ubiquitous commercial traveler. He must prepare his own fuel, and anticipate the want of his plant a year in advance. Wood cutting jobs are to be laid out, and watched to secure a cord of one hundred and twenty-eight cubic feet without too great preponderance of intersticial space, and precautions taken to prevent the labor of months being swept away by the bane of charcoal works—mountain fires.

Then when the ground thaws, and colliers take the place of wood choppers, vigilance is required to secure a proper yield and a good quality of product. Transportation for a bulky friable fuel must be provided, and care bestowed on stocking the the fuel for the months when none is made.

Just when the work for the year is about moving nicely, ominous clouds of smoke rise over the hills, and all hands turn out to participate in a labor, the severity of which only those fully un-understand who have stood in the scorching heat and blinding smoke, with burning thirst, beating back the fire, or cutting a path through briars, which tear clothing and skin, to make a fire line against the roaring sea of flames.

Good generalship is here demanded, coolness and determination are required, backed by the most exacting physical exertion.

The exploitation of the supplies for the furnace requires a partial knowledge of geology, and a familiarity with mining machinery and appliances, and the chemistry and philosophy of the blast furnace need as much study and research from the charcoal founder as from those who operate more pretentious plants with other fuels. The manipulation of loops and blooms demand the same care and attention in the bloomery or forge, as the economic preparation and handling of the puddle ball or muck bar in the rolling mill.

Failures of mining, furnace, or forge machinery are not unfamiliar to the charcoal iron master, and when they come his mechanical ability is sorely taxed to make some temporary arrangement to bridge over the time until the defective part can be replaced from the distant foundry or machine shop.

The account books must be kept with the same care required at larger works, or some wood chopper with his cord tally kept on a peice of sapling, or a forgeman referring to his tonnage as represented by charcoal marks on his kitchen door, will demonstrate their incorrectness.

Purchasing and selling in comparatively small quantities, the market must be carefully studied, and the best possible arrangements secured. In fact, in the charcoal iron business "eternal vigilance is the price of"—success.

That we have not overstated the demands made by the business upon the management of an average charcoal plant we are sure; and yet, with all these varied requirements, the charcoal iron masters being generally distant from one another, have had little opportunity for comparing results obtained, or possible methods of improvement. The mission of the United States Association of Charcoal Iron Workers is to be a medium of communication between those practically engaged in this branch of business, and its usefulness will be developed in proportion to the number of works which unite in it.

We need to investigate forestry in its application to the manufacture of charcoal, and determine where arboriculture is true economy, and what are the merits of various classes of trees when considered prospectively at their maturity.

The various methods of making charcoal also will bear thorough examination, and the use of the meiler, kiln, or retort of various shapes and sizes, can be prcfitably discussed, and practical results compared.

The protection of timber land from ravages by cattle, or from destruction by fire, and the adoption of equitable fence laws are matters of serious importance to all using charcoal.

A résumé of what has been accomplished in collecting and utilizing the acetic vapors arising from the carbonization of wood, an examination of the causes of success or failure, and a consideration of the possible economies which may result from the employment of various processes opens a wide field of investigation.

Methods of transporting, hauling, stocking, and caring for charcoal need exhaustive research.

The employment of charbon roux, or torrefied wood, or the admixture of wood with charcoal, in metallurgical processes, are subjects the consideration of which must be beneficial.

The utilization of saw-mill refuse, saw dust, braize, brands, etc., the coaling of green, dry, or dead wood, the uses of forge, run-out, or furnace cinder, and the adaptation of the raw waste products to the advantage of the trade can be treated with profit to all.

A subject of great importance is the measure and consumption of charcoal.

The shapes, arrangements, and working of various charcoal blast furnaces will form an interesting topic, and a discussion of the merits of hot blast and cold blast would be of value.

The operation of the Catalan forge, and its relaticn to other direct processes, when practically considered, will undoubtedly add to the information of a large class of charcoal iron workers.

The relative economies of using refined metal or raw pig in the forge fires, and the employment of the single or double tuyeres; the construction of forge or run-out fires, hammers, etc., all need more thorough consideration.

The uses of the charcoal iron works product, its especial merit, and its adaptation to certain purposes, is a subject which can profitably receive a share of attention.

With the assistance of the members, and others in the business, the JOURNAL may be made an indispensable feature to every charcoal iron worker. The industry which has been considered as dead or dormant will shew new life, and we will all find that material advancement has followed which will lighten our labors and result in benfit to OURSELVES.

A Large Charcoal Establishment in Sweden.

The new Domnarfvet iron works is located near the ancient mining town of Falon, on the Bergslag railway, in Sweden, and is an extensive charcoal iron works, dependent largely for its fuel upon what, in this country, is usually considered waste.

The power is obtained from the river Dal Elf, and the company also operate saw-mills, which use up 400,000 to 500,000 logs per year. The slabs and refuse are utilized to make a large proportion of the charcoal for the blast furnaces, and the sawdust is used to produce gas for the regenerative furnaces. It is not uncommon to find a Swedish iron works operated in connection with saw-mills, and there is much we can learn from the thorough utilization, of otherwise waste products, in that country.

A description of the works with illustration appeared in the *Iron Age*, of February 19, 1880, from which the following abstract was made: Particular attention is invited to the steep-boshes, pressure of blast, number of tuyeres, and the monolithic hearth of the blast furnaces, the uniformity of product, as evinced by tapping direct into the converter; and the construction of gas producers.

The immense water power is utilized by nine turbines, the construction of which is extremely simple, because the large quantity of bark from numerous saw-mills floating down the river will not permit the use of wheels having guide curves or any system of dividing the wheels. This reduces the duty of the turbines, which it is estimated do not yield more than 55 per cent. of the theoretical maximum. The largest are about 15 feet in diameter. Two four-hundred hourse-power turbines drive the Bessemer blowing engines, two one-hundred-horse-power wheels run the blast furnace blowing engines, one four-hundred-horse-power turbine is used for the heavy plate-mills, one four-hundred-horse-power wheel is set aside for two bar and rail-mills, while three two-hundred-horse-power wheels are used for other mills and machinery.

The ores used analyze from 44.84 to 59.50 per cent. of iron, 0.002 to 0.04 of phosphorus, 0.001 to 0.058 of sulphur; and are carried to the level of the roasting furnaces by means of an inclined plane. The original design included four Westman gas calcining kilns and four blast furnaces, two of each of which are now completed. The blast furnaces, which are placed a little lower than the roasting kilns, are of the ordinary Swedish type of charcoal furnaces, with steep boshes. Their height is 54 Swedish* feet, and the diameter of the boshes 10 feet. The walls of the stack are made of thin fire-brick work, with iron casing, carried by an iron mantle resting upon eight columns. There are six tuyeres, a cinder tap 9 inches below tuyere level, and an iron tap. The hearth and the lower part of the boshes of the blast furnace are made, as usually in Sweden, by ramming a mass of powdered quartz and a little clay around a core. The gas down-comer is about 3 feet in diameter, and terminates in a conical washing box, in which the dust is deposited. The hot-blast stove for each furnace has 2,000 square feet of heating surface, in cast-iron pipes of elliptical section, 14 feet long. The heating gas is burnt in a combustion chamber in front of the stove. When it is considered that the pig made from them is smelted with charcoal, it will be understood why the product is one of great purity.

---

* One Swedish foot=11.69 inches.

The ores are calcined in Westman kilns, broken to the requisite size in crushers. The furnaces are run with blast, having a pressure of 2.4 inches of quicksilver, and heated to about 950° F. The metal is run directly into the Bessemer converters placed below the blast furnaces, about 20 feet in front of them. Of the two converters originally planned, one has now been finished capable of working five-and-a-half-ton charges. The ingots are handled by two ten-ton portable steam cranes. One of the two five-ton open-hearth furnaces originally planned is now built. This furnace is charged with bar ends and Bessemer scrap, which, owing to the low temperature in the converters, cannot be worked in them. For this and many of the other furnaces, sawdust and other refuse is used in gas producers. These are chambers with cylindrical stacks, 7 feet in diameter and about 12 feet high, contracted by a conical fire-box to 4 feet diameter at the bottom, where there is an ordinary fire-grate. The top is covered by a flat brick arch, perforated by a tube, forming the feeding hopper, which is closed by a movable cone of the kind ordinarily used in blast furnaces. An upright pipe in the ash-pit, terminating a little below the level of the grate, serves for the admission of air. The gas produced passes downward by a ractangular channel in the brickwork of the stack to the condenser, a rectangular iron box, about 12 feet long, 2½ feet broad and about 6 feet deep, divided internally, by partitions reaching nearly to the roof and floor alternately, into a series of cells, through which the gas is made to travel in a zig-zag direction, and encounters at the top of each alternate division a series of jets of water, which cool it and remove the steam and other condensable substances with which it may be mingled, and deliver it in a dried state to the main gas-flue, whence it flows into the regenerators in the usual way.

The Bessemer converter is supplied by a two cylinder blowing engine, having a four-foot stroke and cylinders 4 feet in diameter. A second one is now building. One of tho two blowing engines for the blast furnaces is also in operation. The rolling-mill is to contain one three-high bar train, one three-high rod train, one boiler-plate train, one rail train, two trains for tires, and two additional ones for bars and plates. Four of these are now completed, with their reheating furnaces. When completed, the

Domnarfvet works will be one of the largest and best equipped in Sweden. In possession of a large supply of ores of exceptional purity, of an unlimited water-power, cheap fuel and good transportation facilities, these works combine many of the most essential elements of success.

A New Charcoal Forge in Virginia.

By the time the JOURNAL is distributed to the members, an addition to the charcoal iron-works of the country will be in operation at Alexandria, Virginia.

The plant consists of four (4) forge fires, a double heating furnace, a cupola-run-out, steam hammer, and steam-blowing machinery. A portion of the buildings of the locomotive works, located on the Potomac river, in the city of Alexandria, has been adopted for the purposes of the forge.

Four fires are now in place, and two more are to be built. The fires are all cast-iron, without brick linings, and are arranged for working scrap or refined metal. The charging door for metal is on the side. Provision has been made for using two tuyeres, but only one will be employed at the start.

The run-out fire is a decided departure from the ordinary type, and consists of a conical iron structure twelve feet in height, three feet in diameter at the bottom, and two feet in diameter at the top. The bottom is encircled by a water block containing a tapping plate, and above this is a circular Merrit plate, pierced at the back for two tuyeres. The bottom and the sides above the water-block are of fire-brick; the balance of the shaft being lined with red brick. There are charging doors near the bottom and top, a working-door over the tapping plate, and a circular opening below the top, (which is closed,) through which the surplus heat is conveyed to the boiler. The purpose is to use the fire in the ordinary way by charging at the bottom; or, as a cupola fire, by charging near the top, it being the belief of the owners, Messrs. J. P. Agnew & Co., that a considerable economy will result from the employment of the latter method.

In addition to the run out and forge fires there is a double heating furnace. Its novel feature being its construction within an old boiler. The shell acting as buck-staves.

Blast is to be supplied by a horizontal double-acting blowing cylinder, forty-two inches diameter, by sixty-six inches stroke of piston, operated through gearing by a steam-engine, with cylinder fourteen by twenty-four inches. The engine is also to drive shears, &c.

The loops will be shingled under a Miles double-acting steam hammer, with cylinder fourteen inches in diameter, and forty-two inches stroke. The ram weighs three thousand pounds, and strikes upon a ten ton anvil block.

Steam is generated in one plain cylinder-boiler, heated by the forge fires and run-out fire, and a locomotive boiler provided with grate bars, and arranged to utilize the waste heat from the heating furnace.

We shall watch with interest the operation of this forge, as there are so many features different from established precedents.

Remarkable Work in Charcoal Furnaces.

The following data concerning the operation of some of the charcoal blast furnaces is worthy of preservation, and we hope to add, from time to time, good records made at the various charcoal furnaces and forges.

The Bay furnace, 45 feet high and 9½-feet bosh, located at Grand Island, L. S., Michigan, had, up to the spring of 1877, when it was totally destroyed by fire, made the best record for hot-blast charcoal work of any furnace in the country. It was one of the first charcoal furnaces to adopt the bell and hopper and closed front, and was the first charcoal furnace to make 40 tons (2,268 lbs.) in a day, or 1,100 tons in a month.

The Scotia furnace, 40 feet high 9 feet 4 inch bosh, hot-blast, open top, located in Crawford county, Missouri, was built in 1870, and started August 24 of that year. It has been running since that time until February 21, 1880, when it was abandoned, owing to the failure of the ore supply. From the time of starting, it has been stopped only for repairs, and has made 79,500 tons of iron of 2000 pounds per ton. Best month's run 1,171 net tons of iron; yield of ore, 50 per cent. metallic iron; 2 tuyeres, with 5 inch nozzle were used. She has earned a rest by her good record.

The Muirkirk furnace, at Muirkirk, Maryland, 27 feet high and 8⅓ feet across the bosh, hot-blast, open top, three tuyeres, made 72 (2,240 lbs.) tons of car wheel pig iron in one week, in 1878, on lean Maryland ores, of which it took 2¾ tons to make one ton of pig iron.

The Logan furnace, of Valentines & Co., at Bellefonte, Pa., is 8-feet bosh and 35 feet high, open top, blown with cold blast by one tuyere; and made, in 10 months, 3,066 tons of pig iron, consuming per ton of iron 2 1/10 tons ore, 5 cwt. limestone, and 140 bushels of charcoal of 2,150 cubic inches each.

During the month of September, 1879, the Elk Rapids furnace, in Michigan, made, in the four weeks, 316½, 313, 335½, and 336 tons, respectively, a total of 1,301 tons of 2,260 pounds.

The daily out-put during this time averaged 46½ tons, 51½ tons and 42½ tons, being respectively the maximum and minimum.

The furnace is 47 feet high, with 12-feet bosh, hot-blast, and had, up to that time, been in blast 478 days, averaging 39½ tons per day.

The Bangor furnace, at Bangor, Michigan, hot-blast, scant 10-feet bosh, 43 feet high, blown by 3 tuyeres, has made on the present blast, still in continuance, and beginning in May, 1879, an average of over 39½ gross tons of 2,268 pounds per day.

Best month's work, 1,319 tons, (2,268 lbs.;) best week's work, 313 tons; best day's work, 50 tons; yield of ore, 60 per cent.

The latest addition to the charcoal furnaces is the new stack of the Spring Lake Iron Company, at Fruitport, Michigan, 46 feet high, 11-feet bosh, hot-blast, bell and hopper, blown by four tuyeres.

It went into blast March 2, 1880, under the management of H. S. Pickands, Esq., who also made the records above given at Bay and Bangor furnaces. The furnace started off finely. The second week showed a record of 331 gross tons, the third week 343 gross tons, and the fourth week 357 gross tons made in 7 days, with an average consumption of 85¾ bushels of charcoal, the bushel used is 2,748 cubic inches. The ore yielded in furnace 60 per cent.

We can point to the above as truly remarkable records, unexcelled to date, and are pleased that those who accomplished such results are, with one exception, members of the Association.

Greeting.

By Geo. B. Wiestling.

The objects which the United States Association of Charcoal Iron Workers have in view are probably defined with sufficient clearness in the constitution of the Association, to enable every charcoal iron worker to determine as to his sympathy therewith.

An united effort to protect and advance the interests of charcoal iron trade in all its branches, appeals directly to, and affects every charcoal enterprise in our country; while the opportunities and benefits contemplated by the organization, in the mutual interchange of practical and scientific opinions; in the collating of the varied experiences of different operators, and the broad and grand endeavor toward more knowledge of, and greater perfection in, our metallurgical branch, challenges the pride and ambition of every "worker," and will surely enlist the sympathy of all who are of a progressive spirit, and who are untrammeled by the prejudices of ignorance and unrestrained in the ruts of obsoleteness.

It is generally recognized, that the day of "trade secrets" has passed; or, at least, that its policies are as questionable among manufacturers as "trade unions" are among operatives.

The advancing strides in metallurgical practice have been so emphatic, and the ground occupied and in view so comprehensive, that great souls and great minds are to the front, and the minor secrets at separate establishments, are dwarfed and belittled out of thought.

We who recognize our own imperfections are eager to associate with those of more matured experience and advanced thought; while those who excel in metallurgical knowledge, and whose practiced economies have acquired for them the synonym "success," are repaid for their labors and association, by giving to others "what they themselves would receive," and in the further advancement of practical and scientific knowledge.

The executive committee, in sending to the membership this special greeting; strong in our faith that our objects are right, and that only the "right way" in accomplishing our purposes is contemplated; and feeling confident that this must commend itself to every charcoal iron worker in this country, extend the greeting generally, to all engaged in the industry, whether connected with the association or not.

More than one prominent engineer has given expression to the opinion that the days of charcoal iron are numbered. But we believe that the handwriting on the wall exists more in their fancy than in fact.

We advocate no particular special process. We believe that the success of any process in producing *quality* of iron or steel, depends largely on the character of stock employed.

The process may yield a poor article from the best of stock. But we doubt if any process can thus far substantiate the bold claim to ability to eliminate impurities and produce superior quality from impure stocks.

Too often is steel which has been made from ores and metals containing a minimum of impurities pitted in contest against iron, in the manufacture of which, less care was given to the character of the stock employed, and *vice versa.*

By using iron high in phosphorus in the test, it is easily proven that at low temperatures, iron is much weaker than at higher temperatures.

By substituting metal low in phosphorus and high in sulphur, the contrary result may be demonstrated, and finally by using iron neutral in quality, it may be shown that temperature has but slight if any effect upon the metal when undergoing labor.

If ores contain the minimum of impurities which tend to make iron brittle, are necessary to insure good and safe results, so also is the employment of a pure fuel.

We need to have a care that our ore and our flux, compares favorably with the purity of our charcoal as fuel, and that the detail of our processes are such as will not injure quality, and the days of the years of the life of our industry need not be held in apprehension.

We believe that in the blast furnace there are greater possibilities in quantity and quality with charcoal than with any other fuel.

We believe that all other stocks and detail being equal and conditions alike favorable, that better quality results from any process, with charcoal than with any other fuel.

The owner of a charcoal plant, modeled after the plans and advices of metallurgical writers of a decade or more ago, hears with doubts and unbelief, of charcoal blast furnaces of the same dimensions as his own, giving a product three to six times greater than his best results, and with more economy in fuel.

The manager of another establishment, examines the lines and all the detail of other "plants," and wonders "how the thing goes at all."

We *have* persisted in resorting to every means to curb and restrain the process, and then seem astonished at the legitimate result.

We have deliberately planned and constructed our hearths and boshes and lining with everything favorable to their rapid and sure destruction, and their attribute then disappearance to some mysterious agency.

We have designed our lines so that a minimum of blast only is possible, and then conclude that our experience confirms the heresy of some books we have studied on the subject, and that greater density of blast is impossible by reason of the mechanical destruction of the fuel.

We have constructed large forehearths in which to chill our molten iron and form refractory crusts of cinder and iron, and then deem immense bars and "ringers" and "quashes," and woful expenditures of physical labor, essential to the process. Notwithstanding that the use of sand bottoms in puddling and in heating furnaces has been, perforce, abandoned out of respect to quality of product, we have continued the use of sand bottoms in our "runouts," and then conclude the runout a failure.

We have submitted the construction of our fineries, and the "keeping of the same," to those made competent by instructions received from their forefathers, and then we expect the product to be reliable, the economies consulted, and the results comparable with modern processes.

Surely there is abundant call for our organization and its liberal support.

Books of reference on metallurgy are at best behind the age while those which refer particularly to our branch, are few in number, and have proven heterodox in contents.

To whom shall we go? We have the elements within ourselves to insure as marked progress as attaches to any other branch of the business.

We invite the hearty coöperation of all in interest, and again in this first issue of our JOURNAL we extend our kindest "greetings," with profound respect for the past, and abiding faith in the future.

Experiments with Charcoal, Coke, and Anthracite in the Pine Grove Furnace, Pennsylvania.

Although full data concerning the experiments at Pine Grove furnace were published in the proceedings of the American Institute of Mining Engineers and in all the technical journals, the following résumé of them is here given for convenient reference, and to encourage the contribution of other information concerning the comparative value of charcoal and other fuels for furnace use.

In the spring of 1878, the Pine Grove furnace, located in Cumberland county, Pennsylvania, was blown in, after lying idle for several years. The furnace was constructed in 1770, and for over a century it has been in operation. The plant consisted in 1877, of a stone stack thirty-two feet in height, inclosing a shaft and boshes, the latter being nine feet in diameter. The blast was supplied by two wooden blowing tubs discharging into a third, having a floating piston sustaining a box weighted to give the desired pressure, the power being furnished by a water-wheel. A small eighteen-pipe hot-blast stove heated the blast. The furnace was remodeled during the winter of 1877–78, and a Weimer blowing engine, with a blowing tub five feet in diameter and two feet stroke, with the necessary boilers, were substituted for the wooden tubs and water-wheel. The stack was raised, enlarged, and provided with a bell and hopper having a central drop.

Water dam and tymp were added and general repairs made. The hot oven, however, was not increased. The reconstruction was made with a view to continue the use of charcoal, but provision was made for ample blowing capacity should other fuels at any time be employed.

When the charcoal stock was exhausted, on March 22, 1879, Connellsville coke was substituted. The coke charges following immediately upon the last charcoal charges. After working a few days, the strike in the Connellsville coke region cut off the supply, and anthracite coal was obtained, a mixture of the two fuels being employed. The strike continuing, anthracite alone was used until a short time before a new supply of charcoal could be depended upon, when the coke shipments were resumed and mixed fuels again were charged.

The Pine Grove furnace has a bosh nine feet four inches in diameter, and a working height of thirty six feet six inches. The tunnel head is five feet in diameter, closed by bell and hopper, the former being three feet in diameter. The crucible is fifty inches in diameter and five feet in height, pierced for three tuyeres at a height of three feet from the bottom. There is no fore-hearth. The lining and bottom are of fire-brick. The temperature of the blast in all the experiments was between five hundred degrees F. and seven hundred degrees F., the average being six hundred degrees F. It was nearly constant, because, owing to the small size of the oven, it was continually worked to its utmost.

Previous to the use of coke as fuel, the charcoal used was mainly from the stock purchased from a neighboring idle furnace, and was deteriorated by the reloading, hauling by wagons and railroad, and the inclemency of the weather. The consumption, therefore, was above the proper working of the plant; nor was the output as great as it has been. To place results upon as equitable a basis as possible, comparison will be made with the operation of the furnace during the month of February, 1879, the last full month before the change in fuel was made.

When the last charcoal was charged, the furnace was working as follows: Revolutions of engine, 23, equivalent to 1,806 cubic feet per minute; pressure of blast 0.6 pounds, through three 4½-inch nozzles; average product per week, 90 tons. As the coke descended in the shaft of the furnace there was no appreciable difference in the pressure of blast; and at five, P. M., 15 hours after coke was first charged, the revolutions of the engine were increased from 23 to 28, without any increase of pressure. At ten, P. M., the revolutions were 32, and the pressure 1¼ pounds. The following day three 3½-inch nozzles were substituted for the 4½-inch nozzles, which had continued in use up to this time. With the necessary trials to obtain best results, work could not be expected to be very regular, and coke continued to be charged up to April 1, when the record was as follows: Revolutions of engine, 33, equal to 2,592 cubic feet per minute; pressure, 1¼ pounds, through three 3½-inch nozzles. During the ten days coke alone was used, the furnace received 346,000 pounds, or 8,650 bushels of coke; 247.2 tons Pine Grove No. 1 ore, 109.7 tons limestone, and made 99 tons of iron; average pressure of blast, 1 pound, maximum 1¾ pounds.

When it became necessary to use anthracite with the coke, the tuyere nozzles were reduced to 2½ inches; revolutions of engine, 34, equal to 2,670 cubic feet per minute; pressure, 1¾ pounds. In this instance the action of the blast was quite different from that when the coke charges followed those of charcoal, for, as the anthracite descended in the shaft of the furnace, the pressure increased.

The following is a record of the pressure gauge April 2 and 3, 1879:

April 2,	9, P. M.,	revolutions,	34;	pressure,	1¾	pounds.
"	10, P. M.,	"	34;	"	2	"
April 3,	1, A. M.,	"	34;	"	2¼	"
"	3, A. M.,	"	34;	"	2½	"
"	8, A. M.,	"	34;	"	2¾	"
"	10, A. M.,	"	34;	"	3	"
"	12, noon,	"	34;	"	3¼	"

This pressure continued until five, P. M., when the revolutions were increased. A careful estimate showed that the anthracite would be at work at two, P. M., but the maximum pressure at 34 revolutions was reached at noon. The increase due to the resistance of the stock was, therefore, 1½ pounds greater with anthracite mixture than with coke alone. For ten days, up to April 11, the same mixture of fuels was continued. The engine having been run at an average of 35.5 revolutions and an average pressure of 4¾ pounds.

The following is a record of the work with mixed fuels, the average mixture being 81.5 per cent. anthracite, 18.5 per cent. coke: 322,600 pounds anthracite and 73,160 pounds coke, a total of 395,760 pounds fuel consumed in making 112½ tons of iron; 292.3 tons of mixed ores and 145.26 tons limestone were charged in this time. When the last charge of mixed fuels was put into the furnace the fuel was changed to all anthracite. Revolutions of engine, 34; pressure, 4 pounds, through three 2½-inch nozzles. During the time the anthracite was descending through the furnace the pressure increased to 4¾ pounds, demonstrating how a small amount of coke (1-7th) had aided in keeping the furnace "open." With no extraoadinary disturbances the furnace continued on anthracite alone as fuel for 23 days. There was some changes in burden and volume of air, but the quantities were in general constant.

The record of the blast, with anthracite as fuel, is: Average pressure of blast, 4¼ pounds; maximum, 5½ pounds; 331 tons of coal, 480 tons ore, 227.6 tons limestone, 10 tons scrap, which produced 191½ tons of pig iron.

On May 5, the charge of the furnace was made 125 pounds coke and 450 pounds anthracite, (instead of 600 pounds anthracite, which had been the basis up to this time.) Revolutions, 34; pressure, 4¾ pounds. Although no change was made in the speed of the engine, the pressure gradually fell to 3¾ pounds.

On May 10, the proportions of the fuel were changed to 285 pounds anthracite and 285 pounds coke; the pressure gradually fell until at 34 revolutions it was 2½ pounds. Some minor changes in the proportions of coke and anthracite were made to clean up stock, and on May 22, the charge was made 500 pounds of coke, until it, too, was consumed. The operation of the furnace working for the last two days on coke alone, showed a marked decrease in pressure, which at 32 revolutions was 1¾ pounds. Taking the entire period, from May 5 to May 23, as working on mixed fuels, the following results are obtained: Charged 161.4 tons anthracite, 135 tons, or 7,560 bushels, of coke; 460.36 tons Pine Grove No. 2 ore, 3 tons scrap iron, 230.16 tons limestone; 203

tons of pig iron were made. Average pressure of blast, 2½ pounds; maximum, 4¾ pounds.

The anthracite coal used was medium soft, of "steamboat" size. In dividing the various casts of pig iron and crediting them to the different fuels, due allowance was made for the "driving" of the furnace. In estimating this, a given weight of charcoal was assumed as occupying double the space of the same weight of coke, and four times the space of the same weight of anthracite. Allowing for difference in ore and lime burdens, a practically correct estimate was thus made. The most rapid driving of the furnace during February, when running on all charcoal, was 12½ hours; when running on all coke the best day's record showed the stock to have been 20½ hours in the furnace; when using 81½ per cent. anthracite and 18½ per cent. coke, the fastest driving was 22 hours; while with anthracite alone it was 31 hours, and with 55 per cent. anthracite and 45 per cent. coke it was 25 hours.

During the month of August, 1879, the furnace "drove," so that stock did not remain in it but 9½ hours—this was with charcoal as fuel. There was no attempt to make a gray iron for foundry purposes, as the market for the charcoal pig iron is entirely confined to charcoal forges, and for the iron made with anthracite, coke, or mixed fuels, the demand was for mill iron. The records here given are not offered as extraordinary, nor is it claimed that experiments over such brief periods can establish any fair ratio of value for the different fuels. The first ten days, during which coke was used, were partially consumed in trials, and in none of the experiments was the furnace run for a sufficient time to make an equitable comparison. No allowance for leakage was made in calculating the air consumption, and the results obtained are presented more for comparison than to demonstrate the actual amount of air used. There were no defective parts, and the leakages were only such as exist in any furnace in good working order, and those occasioned by snuffing tuyeres, &c., which are difficult to determine.

The following table is merely a recapitulation of data, placed in a convenient form for investigation. All the figures are averaged for the time the fuel memtioned at the head of the columns was used. The tons are 2,260 pounds each for pig iron, 2,240 pounds for everything else:

Summary of results of smelting with charcoal, coke, mixed fuel, and anthracite at the Pine Grove furnace Cumberland county, Pennsylvania.

ITEMS FROM RECORD OF WORKING.	Charcoal, February, 1879.	All coke, March 22 to April 2, 1879.	81.5 per ct. anth., 18.5 per cent. coke, April, 1879.	All anthracite, April and May, 1879.	Anth. 55 per ct., coke 45 per ct., May, 1879.	Charcoal, August, 1879.
Pounds of fuel consumed per ton of pig iron,	2,531	3,494	3,473	3,871	3,271	2,650
Pounds ore and flux carried per pound of fuel,	2.8	2.32	2.47	2.14	2.34	2.64
Tons of iron made per week, average,	95	70	78	58	77	101.6
Percentage of iron yielded in furnace,	38.26	40	38.40	38	43.3	40
Percentage of lime to ore burden,	22	44	50	47.4	50	24.4
Average cubic feet of blast per minute	1,896	2,435	2,749	2,434	2,473	2,301
Average cubic feet of air per ton of iron,	197,084	323,845	338,187	398,679	317,170	216,243
Average cubic feet of air per pound fuel,	77.8	92.66	96.13	103	97	81
Average pressure of blast in pounds,	0.77	1.	4.25	4.75	2.5	1.25
Tuyere area in square inches.	47.7	28.9	14.7	14.7	14.7	42.5
Least time that stock was in furnace, hours,	12.5	20.5	22	31	25	9.5
Grade of iron,	2.4	3	2 7	3	3	2
Duration of experiments, days,	28	10	10	23	19	31

A Bushel of Charcoal.

It would seem that the height of meterological folly had been reached when the manager of a charcoal forge buys 2,000 pounds of coke for his run-out fire, 2,240 pounds of anthracite for his household uses, 2,268 pounds of pig iron for his forge, sells 2,464 pounds of blooms credits his run-out with 2,700 pounds of refined metal, and in his books charges up each of these individual amounts as A TON. But when we investigate what is meant by a bushel of charcoal we meet confusion worse confounded, and the problem of determining some standard would seem impossible of solution. In a paper read at the Lake George meeting of the American Institute of Mining Engineers, in 1878, we called attention to this matter in the following manner:

"In making the comparison of the operation of various charcoal furnaces, the writer has found difficulty in arriving at proper conclusions, owing to the variety of bushels in use. They have been found to be rated in capacity from 2,150 to 2,748 cubic inches, and in weight from 16 to 22.5 pounds. Two works in one neighborhood have been noted, where the standards were respectively the two extremes of weight mentioned, although the timber used was of the same varieties and proportions.

"It has, therefore, been necessary to reduce the fuel consumed per ton of iron to cords of wood, as a cord seems to represent a fixed quantity in all districts, except so far as the ingenuity displayed in piling by woodchoppers affects its interstitial spaces."

Since this paper was presented, further inquiry has developed still greater variation, and lately, for the use of the members of the Association, an effort has been made to collect all statutes and legislative enactments in existence throughout the different States. To accomplish this purpose, letters were addressed to the various Secretaries of State, most of whom have cheerfully furnished the information desired.

From these responses we learn that Maine, Vermont, New Jersey, Delaware, Maryland, Virginia, Alabama, Mississippi, Texas, Kentucky, Arkansas, Ohio, Indiana, Illinois, Michigan, and Wisconsin have no legislative enactment regulating the sale of charcoal. Maine delegates this privilege to each town. Maryland has no statute but the Baltimore city code. Section 44, page 530, provides that "the standard for a bushel of charcoal shall be $2,747\frac{70}{100}$ cubic inches, full allowance for a cone or heaped measure."

Section 17, chapter 121, of general laws of New Hampshire, says: "Every basket or other measure by which charcoal shall be measured or sold shall be not less, in its average diameter, than twenty inches, and of a depth sufficient to contain eighteen gallons level measure, which shall be accounted two bushels, or one strike."

At 231 cubic inches per gallon, the stand and bushel is 1,989 cubic inches, without heaping.

General statutes of Massachusetts, 1860, chapter 49, section 191, is as follows: In the sale of charcoal, the baskets, tubs, or vessels used in measuring the same, except as hereinafter provided, shall be of a cylindrical form, and of the following dimensions in the inside thereof, to-wit: nineteen inches in diameter in every part, and eighteen inches and one tenth of an inch in depth, measured from the highest part of the bottom thereof; each of which shall be deemed to be of the capacity of two bushels, and shall be filled level full. * * * * * *

Section 192. Charcoal may be measured in boxes, bins, or cans, of the following capacities, to-wit: of five, ten, twenty, thirty, forty, or fifty bushels, such boxes, bins, or cans being first lawfully sealed; and five thousand one hundred and thirty-two cubic inches shall be deemed equal to two bushels, or the level basket, tub, or vessel described in the preceding section.

Section 193 fixes penalty of ten dollars for having possession of any other measure than the above, and the destruction of the vessel and a forfeiture of not more than fifty cents for each bushel of charcoal measured in such irregular measure, except by special agreement between buyer and seller.

Section 194 provides for appointment of suitable person to see to enforcement of above provisions.

The standard bushel of Massachusetts is therefore 2,566 cubic inches.

General statues of Rhode Island, (revision of 1872,) chapter 116, section 4: Every basket used in measuring charcoal brought into any town for sale shall be of the following dimensions, to wit: Nineteen inches in breadth in every part thereof, and seventeen and one half inches deep, measuring from the highest part of the bottom of the basket perpendicularly to a level with the top of the basket. The contents of such a measure level full, are 4,961.6 cubic inches if made round, or 6,317.5 cubic inches if made square.

(By sections 5 and 6, charcoal can only be measured in baskets of the above size.)

Title 16, chapter 15, section 8, general statutes of Connecticut: In the sale of charcoal and all other articles sold by heaped measure 1,282 cubic inches shall constitute a half bushel, 2,564 cubic inches is therefore the standard.

The New York statutes do not refer especially to charcoal, but it is probably covered by the law which reads:

"The standard half bushel shall contain 1,075.21 cubic inches.

"The measure of capacity for coal, ashes, marl, &c., &c., shall be the half bushel, and its multiple and sub-divisions, and the measures used to measure such commodities shall be made cylindrical, with plain and even bottoms, and shall be of the following diameters from outside to outside: the bushel 19½ inches, half bushel 15½ inches, peck 12⅓ inches."

That is, giving the outside diameter of the bushel measure, and the cubic contents of the half bushel, one may figure out the inside diameter and inside height of the bushel for himself. Presumably, it must contain 2,150.42 cubic inches.

A statue of Pennsylvania, dated January 22, 1847, (see pamphlet laws of that year, page 51,) specifies that "the standard measure of charcoal shall be 2,571 cubic inches for each and every bushel thereof."

The revised statues of Missouri, 1879, section 7667, provided under act of March 25, 1868, that "the measure shall be for coke and charcoal 2,680 cubic inches for every bushel."

In Montana there is no standard fixed by territorial statue for the bushel of charcoal. The United States Government, a pretty large buyer, allows 2,650 cubic inches for a bushel, and all their purchases are on that basis. The measurement allowed by all other buyers varies from 2,500 to 2,650 cubic inches, governed by the respective needs of buyer and seller. Probably 2,550 cubic inches is the usual measurement obtained by the general purchaser.

The revised statutes of Minnesota, 1866, chapter 21, section 6. states that "Every basket or other measure by which charcoal is sold shall not be less in its average diameter than 20 inches, and of sufficient depth to coutain 4,839 cubic inches, which shall be accounted two bushels."

The standard is therefore 2,419½ cubic inches.

In California charcoal is sold by the pound, or by the net ton.

Oregon has no standard. The Oswego Iron Company use the very liberal bushel of 2,844 cubic inches.

Now how are we to compare the economies of our work as to fuel consumption when there is such a variation in our legislative enactments. We have data from iron works using bushels of from 2,150 to 2,844 cubic inches, and a plant employing 132⅓ of the smaller bushels to make a ton of pig iron would be doing as well as the Oswego furnace using but 100 bushels of the larger measure. But in States where there is a statute fixed by-law, there is generally a clause making it inoperative bv contract, and it is an unusual thing to find an iron works employing the State standard. Thus in Pennsylvania, where the statute provides for a bushel of 2,571 cubic inches, we lately visited four charcoal iron works, which could all be seen in a continuous drive of an hour, and found that although the ores used were the same, that cold blast was blown at each furnace, that each had its own forge, that all coal was measured, not weighed, and that there was a uniformity unusual for neighboring plants, the bushel of charcoal employed were respectively 2,150, 2,250, 2,675, and 2,690 cubic inches.

We shall continue the discussion of the bushel in our next JOURNAL, and will take up the different weights employed, and a comparison of the two methods of measurement now used.

The Chilling Properties of Cast-iron.

What makes a chilled iron has been a conundrum for many years, and it is even now not definitely solved; but recent investigations point to the chemical constituents as the true cause, and a certain compound of carbon and silicon (the exact composition of which is unknown) as the principal factor.

It has lately been demonstrated tnat the presence of graphitic or free carbon in cast iron is the predominating cause which prevents it welding and now, we learn that the combined carbon with silicon in cast-iron influences its chilling properties. Mr. John L. Gill, Jr., of Pittsburgh, Pa., a manufacturer of car wheels, determined to investigate the chilling properties of various irons, and went to considerable expense, erecting an experimental cupola, constructing an elaborate testing machine, and establishing a laboratory. He made a large number of experiments as to the chemical and physical properties of numerous irons as affecting their chill.

To Mr. S. A. Ford, chemist of the Edgar Thomson Steel Works, who carried out the analytical work for Mr. Gill, we are indebted for an interesting letter, detailing his researches to determine the effect the chemical composition of irons have upon their chilling proprieties.

Mr. Ford's investigations indicate that this unknown compound of silicon and carbon has a great influence on the wearing property (or hardness) of a piece of chilled iron; that wheels which had made the greatest mileage contained the most of this compound; and that this compound was formed in certain irons when suddenly cooled.

In the various irons which he examined, Mr. Ford found that all the silicon in white irons (that is, iron made in a cold furnace) was soluble in hydrochloric acid; that part of the silicon in gray irons was soluble, and part was precipitated in light flocculent particles, intermingled with graphite, and that in chilled irons all or nearly all of the silicon is insoluble, and its precipitate is more compact and essentially different from that of gray iron; and this difference is more decidedly shown by further treatment with potash.

Mr. Ford found that the irons which, before chilling, had the greatest amount of soluble silicon contained, after chilling, the largest amount of this insoluble silicon. Analyses of irons from the same wheel show that of the total silicon 29 per cent. was insoluble in the gray iron and 60 per cent. was insoluble in the chilled iron.

That this peculiar insoluble silicon affects the hardness of a chill was demonstrated by analyses like the following:

A wheel which made a mileage of 71,000 showed that 90 per cent. of the total silicon existed as this compound, while but 10 per cent. was found in a wheel which had been able to run only 12,000 miles.

In three wheels of different makes, which had each run 48,000 miles, this insoluble silicon represented in each case 34 per cent. of the total.

Further experiments demonstrated that gray iron, which gave the largest amount of insoluble silicon, with flocculent precipitate, produced the poorest chill, while those having the greatest amount of soluble silicon gave the hardest chill, and the chill contained the most of the insoluble silicon, (or compound,) with compact precipitate. Analysis of a gray iron, which gave a very soft or "zinc" chill, showed 59 per cent. of the silicon to be insoluble, and an analysis of a gray iron, which produced a hard and perfect chill, but 29 per cent. of the silicon was insoluble.

Mr. Ford sums up his researches by expressing as his conviction that, irons which contain the most of that form of silicon which is soluble in dilute hydrochloric acid will form the hardest and best chill, and that this hardness is mainly due to the amount of this supposed compound of carbon and silicon. The greater the proportion of this compound the longer the service of the wheel.

We thus have a test which will aid in determining the relative values of irons for car wheel purposes, and trust to soon be able to publish more information on the subject.

The Denudation of our Forests.

The large area of woodland which is annually cleared to produce fuel for the various charcoal iron works of the country would indicate that but a few years of existence are still granted to the industry. Such, undoubtedly, will be the case if only stumpage or wood-leave is purchased; but as many thousands of acres (the aggregate of which we expect to give in another issue of the Journal) are owned by the various charcoal iron establishments, and as it is the policy of these works to maintain a supply of timber for future use, we are really the only trade organization whose interest it is to encourage the growth of forests.

The saw-mills use immense quantities of lumber, but, when a tract is cleared, the interest of the operator in the growth of the timber ceases. So with the seeker after railroad sills or fence-posts and rails, either of which draw more heavily on the woodlands of the country than is generally believed. But the charcoal iron works encourage the growth of timber; they protect, as far as the peculiar fence laws of the land permit, the young sprouts from roving cattle; they utilize the force of employés to stop the ravages of the forest fires; thus annually preserving from destruction a vast acreage of woodland.

Dr. Hough, in his able report on forestry, in 1877, makes the following comments on fences:

"In no branch of rural economy is there so much needless waste of forest products as in fencing, and in nothing is there so much need of reform. The costly practice of fencing cattle *out* of fields, where not wanted, instead of *in* fields, where they should be kept, would become apparent by a simple calculation, and the economy of inclosing large fields, instead of small ones, may be easily shown.

"In the prairie States, farmers have found from necessity that it is cheaper to tether their domestic animals, if few, or to herd them, if many, than it is to inclose their range with fences.

"Estimates have been made, showing the cost of fences in the United States to be $1,700,000,000, and the annual cost of maintenance $198,000,000, including interest, at 6 per cent., upon the original cost."

So great has been the consumption of timber for fence purposes that the newer wire fences became a necessity. To show the quantity of wire used for fences, the following was clipped from the newspapers:

"The Gautier Steel Company has made contracts, since January 1, to supply barb-fence manufacturers, before June, with wire to the amount of more than $1,000,000. It is said that over 50,000 miles of plain wire will be barbed and put on the market this year."

This, of course, represents an immense saving of timber, probably, 150,000 cords.

Railroad sills require the denudation of fully 30,000 acres of woodland annually, for taking the aggregate length of railroads in the country at 85,000 miles, and allowing 2,500 sills to the mile, each sill being made from a stick 8 inches in diameter and 8 feet long, and estimating the life of the sill at 7 years, we have an annual consumption, taking only the part of the tree used for sills of 8 cords per mile, or a total of 680,000 cords per year.

It is imposible at present to get at the amount of timber used for sills to go out of the country, but it is a matter of great importance for immense numbers are shipped from our Atlantic ports to England and other foreign countries.

The exportation of lumber is also growing to large proportions, both from eastern and western ports. The manufacture and shipment of lumber is the leading industry of western Oregon and Washington, much of the magnificent forests of that country yielded from 250,000 to 1,000,000 feet per acre, finding a market in East India, Europe, Japan, China, etc.

The manufacturer of wood pulp consumes no inconsiderable quantity of timber, and if we add this to the lumber, fence and sill demand, and the quantity used for firing boilers, locomotives, and for household purposes, we will find that although the charcoal iron industries uses annually a tremendous aggregate of timber, it clears but a limited proportion of the acreage annually denuded.

It is estimated that since 1835, the forest area of the western hemisphere has decreased at the average rate of 7,600,000 acres or nearly 12,000 square miles per annum. In the United States it was at the rate of 1,600 square miles in 1835, 7,000 square miles in 1855, 8,400 square miles in 1876, and probably 9,000 square miles in 1879.

A large quantity of the charcoal consumed is made from slabs, etc., from saw-mills and the smaller wood after the larger has been utilized for other purposes. Twenty per cent. of the charcoal used is estimated as made from this discarded material.

The consumption of wood for charcoal iron works last year, was, probably, 1,400,000 cords, deducting 20 per cent. as above, we have a total of 1,120,000 cords, which at an allowance of 28 cords per acre, required the clearing of 40,000 acres of woodland, or say 7 per cent. of the total denudation of the year, but, probably, 75 per cent. of this area, or 30,000 acres, will be continued as timber land, while of the immense acreage cleared for other purposes it is doubtful if over 10 per cent. will grow up as woodland.

The large tracts of forest land maintained by the charcoal iron works are of incalculable benefit to the country by the beneficial climatic effects which they produce, and the influence they exert on the water powers, the growth of crops, and the public health. For to maintain a permanent supply of charcoal, an iron works must maintain 25 to 30 acres of wood land for every acre cleared.

In an editorial on the value of forests, the Philadelphia Star says:

"Those who have given this subject thought are familiar with the fact that denuding a country of its natural forests tends to cause droughts. The planting of trees has been suggested as a remedy; it is of the first importance to the entire country and especially that portion west of the Alleghenies, where the prairies occupy so large a space."

"The constantly recurring droughts, the drying up cf rivers, and the general scarcity of water in that section long since should have shown its inhabitants that in the wholesale slaughtering of their forests they were simply preparing for sterility of soil and consequently failure of crops. The cultivation of the soil also affects its humidity, and therefore there seems to be no other alternative than to set vigorously to work planting trees to replace the ones cut away."

"It used to be that barns in Ohio were removed in order to get away from the manure heaps, and where rivers were convenient the accumulations of the barn-yard were carted away and dumped into them. It is not the case now. Fertilizers of every kind are in constant demand, and yet those supposed to be inexhaustible soils are very far from producing such crops as when they were poorly cultivated."

"Just so with trees. Forests that a quarter of a century since were regarded as worse than worthless would, were it possible to replace them, be worth ten times as much as the now cultivated lands on which they stood. We shall be taught wisdom by experience in this matter, and the sooner the lessons are thoroughly impressed on the minds of western farmers the better it will be for them."

The same reasoning is equally applicable to eastern and southern States.

But while we can claim credit for the charcoal iron trade for propagating forests, we cannot extol it for the care bestowed upon the growing woodland, nor for the economical use of the wood obtained from it.

Of the 30,000 acres cleared last year and allowed to return to timber, but little, if any, of it will receive other attention than occasionally driving away stray cattle or keeping fires from destroying it entirely. The 2,000,000 or more cords of wood which will be made into charcoal during 1880, will make no more iron than could be obtained from the use of 900,000 cords, if the economies of proper carbonization, improved construction, and thorough management were more carefully studied, and the results obtained at different works intelligently compared.

As long as 100 pounds of wood are used to obtain 18 to 20 pounds of charcoal, which is about a fair average, we are far from securing an equivalent value for the wood consumed, and while an average of 4 cords of wood are consumed to make a ton of pig iron, or of Catalan blooms, and 3 cords or more to make a ton of blooms from refined metal or raw pig, we are not approaching the practical results possible with continuous processes, modern plants, etc., and judicious management.

There is no more reason why primitive methods should continue in the manufacture of charcoal than in the production of coke. The improved appliances and processes employed have done more to introduce coke into the extended use it now enjoys as a metallurgical fuel than anything else. There are just as great economic possibilities before the manufacturer of charcoal as the coke producer has found, and labor saving appliances, as well the erection of proper structures for carrying on the process so as to obtain the fullest results from the material used, will yield as good fruit to us as to others.

We are rapidly approaching the time when steps will be taken to preserve our timbered area, and before the new century enters, we shall, probably, have in this country an organized action by the various States or General Government to encourage forestry. Already we find thought devoted to the waste products. Sawdust is being converted into pyroligneous acid; in Sweden as we have shown on pages 13 and 15 it is employed to produce gas for regenerative furnaces. A few days ago a United States patent was granted to make railroad ties, fence posts, paving and building blocks, etc., out of sawdust. This artificial wood, it is claimed, can be made fire and water proof, and no insects will attack it. It will take a high polish and stand a higher pressure than ordinary wood. It also can be cut and sawed and will allow of nails being driven into it.

Metal is largely displacing wood in constructive work, and many economies are being practiced where wood is becoming scarce.

Judicious attention bestowed on the forests to insure good timber will bring with it a return scarcely appreciated now; and an expenditure of a small amount annually in the care of forests will earn good interest.

We believe a candid investigation into the comparative merits of kilns and open pits for coaling wood, will demonstrate that allowing for interest on cost of construction, expense of hauling wood, etc., and crediting the saving of wood resulting from the better yield obtained, kilns are preferable in a majority of cases, and their value is constantly increasing. Notwithstanding the oft-repeated assertion that kiln coal is inferior to meiler or pit coal, we find that the plants doing the best work and using the least amount of charcoal per ton of iron, use kiln coal largely.

We go further and state our belief that in the very near future, the now waste acetic vapors resulting from wood carbonization will be collected, and by being reduced to a commercial product, largely diminish the cost of making charcoal in many iron works.

We expect our friend A to smile incredulously, and tell us how B's kilns proved unsuccessful and were abandoned, or how C burned up all the wood he put in his; and our co-laborer X to advise us not to go too fast, for Y and Z both tried retorts and endeavored to collect acetic vapors, but the experiment ruined them financially.

We know all this, and we know, too, that the most assured success results from failures. We also know that for every cord of wood "burned up" in kilns, hundreds of cords have been wasted in meilers, and that immense importations of commercial acetates enter our ports, every pound of which can be made in our own country from the vapors arising from wood carbonization for charcoal iron works.

Surely the economies possible, are worthy of careful study and thorough investigation; an interchange of data concerning both successful and disastrous experiences is what is most needed NOW.

Through the courtesy of Mr. P. L. Weimer we are able to present a cut of the steam blowing apparatus he has just completed for the Port Oram, N. J., forge. There are two vertical blowing cylinders, each 40 inches in diameter, and 24 inches stroke, operated through a crank shaft from a horizontal steam cylinder 14 inches in diameter, and 18 inches stroke. The maximum speed is 125 revolutions per minute, the ordinary working speed 100

PAT. AUG 22' 1876
P.L. WEIMER
LEBANON PA.

revolutions, discharging 7,000 cubic feet of air, or 70 cubic feet per revolution.

A similar arrangement of blowing cylinders, operated by a belt wheel on the shaft, and driven by a turbine wheel, are in use at the Carlisle iron-works, Pa. The blowing cylinders are, however, 30 inches in diameter, and 18 inches stroke, delivering 2,900 cubic feet of air per minute, at 100 revolutions. At a very regular pressure, they can be worked up to 4 pounds pressure.

The Charcoal Industry of the United States.

We very much regret that it is impossible to fulfill the promise made in the circular issued and present a report upon the industry, giving the number of charcoal iron works in each State, with the acreage of farm and timber lands, number of employés, etc, but such a paper, unless complete, would be of little value. Although a large amount of data has been collected, there are "missing links" without which the report would not be exhaustive. By deferring its publication the data can be compared with the statistics collected by the American Iron and Steel Association and its value thereby enhanced. Under the circumstances we considered it best to postpone the paper than to longer delay this issue of the journal. We append as an apology some extracts from the paper read at the September meeting of the association with other data, as preliminary to the report which we expect to present shortly in another issue of the journal.

The first record of the amount of iron made is in 1810, when there were in existence in this country 153 charcoal furnaces, 135 bloomaries, 330 forges, and 34 rolling and slitting-mills, producing 53,908 gross tons of pig iron and 36,385 tons of blooms, billets, and bars. In 1840 the number had been increased to 804 furnaces, producing 286,903 gross tons of cast iron, and 795 forges, bloomaries, and rolling-mills. As the use in the blast furnace of anthracite coal, or of coke made from bituminous coal, or of raw bituminous coal, had not been commercially successful prior to 1838, it is evident that by far the larger portion of the iron made up to that time was produced with charcoal as fuel.

From 1840 there has been what is usually termed a decadence of the charcoal iron industry; it is, however, more of an overshadowing. Many of the furnaces, forges, and bloomaries which were in operation in 1840 are permanently abandoned. Some of these works were forced to cease operations by reason of the denudation of forest lands, and their conversion into arable tracts; while others, owing to their location being distant from a suitable ore supply or from railroad facilities, have been unable to compete in the market with plants more favorably situated. But the charcoal iron industry is at present of more importance than is generally accredited to it, and is likely to hold its place, at least until such time as the value of timber is sufficiently enhanced to make its utilization for other purposes than producing charcoal more important than at present.

A comparison of the charcoal iron product of various years shows that in 1874 more than double the amount of charcoal pig iron was made than in 1840, and that even in the depressed times of 1877 and 1878 the quantity produced each year was in excess of that reported for 1840, when the decline of the industry is usually considered to have commenced. From 1840 to 1850 the total pig iron product increased 96½ per cent., and the use of natural fuels was undoubtedly the main stimulus for this increase; yet more than one half of the 564,755 net tons of pig iron made in 1850 was produced with charcoal as fuel. The quantity of of pig iron made with charcoal was in excess of the amount made with anthracite coal until 1855, and the output of the furnaces using bituminous coal and coke was less than the product of those using charcoal for fuel until 1869.

In 1873, under the impetus of high prices, there was more charcoal iron made *than ever before;* and 577,620 net tons were produced; being 20 per cent. of the whole output of pig iron for the year.

Pig iron represents but a portion of the charcoal iron industry, and, to demonstrate the condition and capacity of other branches of the business, the following table has been prepared, which illustrates the fluctuations in the production of bloomaries and forges from 1865 to 1878, and the relations borne to the rolled iron made and the output of the Bessemer and Siemens-Martin steel plants.

Years.	Net tons of blooms and billets made.	Net tons of Bessemer and open-hearth steel ingots made.	Net tons of iron rolled.	Net tons of charcoal pig iron made.	Net tons of all other pig iron made.
1865, ...	63,977	. . . . . .	†856,340	†262,342	†669,240
1866, ...	73,555	. . . . . .	1,026,089	332,580	1,017,763
1867, ...	73,073	†3,400	1,039,396	344,341	1,117,285
1868, ...	*75,200	9,500	1,097,775	370,000	1,233,000
1869, ...	69,500	12,500	1,226,356	392,150	1,524,491
1870, ...	62,259	45,000	1,291,000	365,000	1,500,000
1871, ...	63,000	51,000	1,447,483	385,000	1,526,608
1872, ...	58,000	123,108	*1,847,922	500,587	*2,353,971
1873, ...	62,564	174,152	1,837,430	*577,620	2,290,658
1874, ...	61,670	198,933	1,694,616	576,557	2,112,856
1875, ...	49,243	384,567	1,599,516	410,990	1,855,591
1876, ...	†44,628	547,486	1,509,296	308,649	1,784,587
1877, ...	47,300	585,618	1,476,759	317,843	1,996,742
1878, ...	50,045	*768,352	1,555,576	293,399	2,282,962

* Maximum. † Minimum.

No estimates are presented for 1879, for we prefer giving exact figures in another issue.

Bessemer steel was first made a commercial success in this country in 1865, and the Siemens-Martin process was introduced in 1868; in 1878 there were produced by these two systems 758,352 net tons of steel ingots. As the amount of rolled iron has increased since 1864, and the forges and bloomaries have not been seriously crippled, it is plain that these steels have made their own market, and filled a place in trade not formely provided for. The peculiar properties they possess have to a large extent encouraged an increase of trade, but undoubtedly much of the production of the steel works, without their existence, would have been supplied by forges or bloomaries and rolling-mills.

A *resumé* of the charcoal industry of to-day is as follows: There are 260 blast furnaces distributed through 22 States. Of these, 86, located in 17 States, were active in 1878, making on an average 3,500 net tons of iron each. Of the furnaces which were not operated, some, owing to location, will not again be put in blast, and the maximum capacity of the charcoal furnaces in the country approximates 700,000 net tons per annum, or about one eighth of the total blast furnace capacity. There are now in existence 58 bloomaries and 64 Catalan forges, with an aggregate capacity of 125,000 net tons per annum.

Calculating the output in 1878 of the furnaces, steel works, forges, bloomaries, and rolling-mills as percentages of the possible production, the results are as follows: 42 per cent. of the charcoal furnace capacity, 40 per cent. of the forge and bloomary capacity, 43 per cent. of the rolling-mill capacity, 46 per cent. of the bituminous coal furnace capacity, 48 per cent. of the anthracite coal furnace capacity, and 90 per cent. of the Siemens-Martin and Bessemer steel works capacity were active in 1878. The above percentages are less than they really should be, for it is altogether improbable that all the iron works would be in condition to operate at one time, but they demonstrate that the amount of business done by the charcoal iron industry compared more favorably with the other branches than is generally supposed during the depression from which we are emerging.

The Hanging-Rock Region.

One of the most interesting districts in the country to the charcoal iron-worker, is that portion of the States of Ohio and Kentucky, embracing Lawrence, Jackson, Gallia, Vinton, Hocking, and part of Perry counties in the former, and Greenup, Boyd, Carter, and Lawrence counties in the latter. It extends seventy-five miles north and forty-five miles south of the Ohio river, covering an area of about two thousand square miles.

The name was obtained from a cliff, some four hundred feet in height, on the Ohio side of the river, the upper portion of which projects like the cornice of a building.

The first effort to produce iron was made in 1815, by one Richard Deering, who erected a cupola in Greenup county, Kentucky, the success of which induced him, and others who joined him, to erect a furnace in 1818–19, on the Little Sandy river, six miles from Greenupsburg, in the same county. The stack was twenty-five feet high, and six feet bosh, "*cut solid in a cliff of black slate, hence called 'Argilite,' with only two sides for tyrup and tuyere arches.*" An undershot wheel, driven by the water of the river, furnished power for the blast. The iron made was run into hollow-ware on week-days, and into pigs on Sundays.

In 1824, the Pactolus furnace was built in the same county,

and others followed, until eighty-four furnace stacks have been built in the region.

At present, there are over forty charcoal furnaces in existence in the area described above, with an aggregate daily capacity of five hundred tons hot blast, and eighty tons cold blast, pig iron.

In 1837, the first hot blast stove was erected at Vesuvius furnace, by the late William Firmstone, Esq.

In 1844, Mr. Robert Hamilton, the sole proprietor of Pine Grove furnace, made the experiment of stopping that furnace on the Sabbath, which, notwithstanding the contrary prediction of his friends, proved successful, and the custom at this day is very generally adopted throughout the region.

The commercial centers for the charcoal iron works are at Ironton, in Ohio, and Greenupsburg, Kentucky, and the character of the iron made has been such as to achieve a most enviable reputation. The charcoal furnaces work almost exclusive with open top and hot blast; the machinery being driven by steam, and use, principally, the local ores. An interesting description of the region is published in the History of Ohio, from which these notes were, in part, obtained.

The Price of Charcoal Irons.

Reports from over fifty iron works, dated April 1, show comparatively light stocks on hand, the aggregate being 11,200 tons pig iron; a very small quantity of blooms are in the hands of the makers.

The advices received from the New England States place car wheel irons at $56 and $58, Catalan blooms at $68 and $72.

Pennsylvania car wheel irons are closely sold up at $55 at works with some orders ahead.

The hot-blast irons range from $40 to $46. Plate charcoal blooms are selling at $95 at works, and anthracite run-out blooms at $80 to $83 50.

Maryland car wheel hot blast may be quoted at $60: We have one report of sale of furnace product for April and May at $65@6 months delivered in Baltimore.

Virginia blooms sell at about same rate as quoted for those in Pennsylvania.

Alabama hot-blast irons are reported at $33 to $35; cold blast $45.

The Hanging Rock, Ohio irons, bring $30 to $40 for hot-blast, $60 to $65 for cold blast car wheel irons.

About 2,000 tons are reported in stock in the Kentucky Hanging Rock region, the prices ranging from $36 to $41 for hot blast, and $58 to $62 for cold blast car wheel irons, 4 months.

The Lake Superior furnaces reported prices for hot-blast irons at say $50—7,500 tons being sold at prices ranging from $50 to $52 50, one furnace refused an offer of $48 for product of furnace to July 1.

The market is quiet, and demand less active than a month ago. A large number of furnaces will not go into blast for a month or more. Yet there is a probability of a decrease in price of pig iron and blooms, owing to the unexpected weakening of the general iron market.

JOHN BIRKINBINE,
Secretary United States Association of Charcoal Iron Workers.

John C. Trautwine, C. E., contributes to the *Franklin Institute Journal* the results of experiments made to determine the shearing strengths of some American woods, as adapted to pins or tree-nails.

The following is a summary of the results in pounds per square inch of cross section:

Ash,	6,280	Hickory,	6,045 7,285
Beech,	5,223		
Birch,	5,595	Maple,	6,355
Cedar, (white,)	1,372 1,519	Oak, (white,)	4,425
		Oak, (live,)	8,480
Cedar, (Central American,)	3,410	Pine, (white,)	2,480
		Pine, (northern yellow,)	4,340
Cherry,	2,945	Pine, (southern yellow,)	5,735
Chestnut,	1,536	Pine, (very resinous yellow,)	5,053
Dogwood,	6,510	Poplar,	4,418
Ebony,	7,750	Spruce,	3,255
Gum,	5,890	Walnut, (black,)	4,728
Hemlock,	2,750	Walnut, (common,)	2,830
Locust,	7,176		

The Association.

We feel considerable pride in publishing in the journal a list of members of the Association, and have good reason for gratification at the favor with which the organization has been received by the trade generally, as evidenced by the uniform courtesy extended to it in replies given to inquiries sent out by the Secretary. We gratefully acknowledged this interest, and have but a single interest to record, where information has been refused, this would not be mentioned, except as a contrast to show the generous response of the rest of the trade.

When we remember how widely dispersed the charcoal iron works are, and consider the traditional conservatism characteristic of the management of many of these industries, we can not anticipate a stampede into the organization, particularly when some of the associations of kindred industries are maintained to "bull" prices, or establish card rates which are invariably discounted or shaded by the members, or prepare sliding scales whose effect seems to be to give the employés the *ipse dixit* in the operation of the works.

What we did look for, and what we expect, is a gradual healthy growth, which will represent the entire charcoal iron interest in the Association.

Our membership now extends into sixteen States, and embraces within it names which have become renowned in the trade by the large output of the works they control, and the results obtained with small consumption of fuel. The membership includes representatives of industries whose brand of iron is a synonym of superiority. It embraces catalan forges and bloomeries, where raw pig, cold or hot [illegible] run-out metal is used, and whose product enters into all the various special uses peculiar to the business.

Blast furnaces using cold and hot blast, and producing malleable, chilling, or steel irons, are already represented; and among those composing the Association, are operators who employ a variety of methods and structures for producing charcoal.

The association of so many who have helped to advance the charcoal iron business, having a common purpose to improve the industry, cannot but be beneficial, and the interchange of views, through the medium of the organization, must result in value to all who share in its benefits.

In the organization an endeavor was made to place its advantages within the reach of every charcoal iron works, without being a burden, and the annual fee was fixed at ten dollars, with this end in view. There is no expensive features connected with its management, and the net receipts are devoted to the benefit of the members.

We can, therefore, commend to all interested in the trade, the Association and its purpose, which is distinctly stated in the preamble of the constitution, elsewhere published, and would invite every charcoal iron-worker in the country to unite with it.

In the JOURNAL we shall endeavor to give an idea of the extent of the charcoal iron industry of the country. Surely its magnitude is sufficient to sustain a strong organization whose influence shall extend throughout the land.

List of Members United States Association of Charcoal Iron Workers.

John P. Agnew, Alexandria, Va.
Park Agnew, Alexandria, Va.
H. W. Bates, Riverton, Greenup county, Ky.
Irving M. Beam, Milwaukee, Wis.
John Birkinbine, Pine Grove Furnace, Pa.
Seymour Brownell, Duluth, Minn.
Edw. S. Buckley, Gray's Ferry Iron Works, Philadelphia.
Charles Campbell, Ironton, Lawrence county, Ohio.
John Campbell, Ironton, Lawrence county, Ohio.
Charles E. Coffin, Muirkirk, Prince George's county, Md.
Geo. D. Colby, Katahdin Iron Works, Maine.
Jay Cooke, 112 South Third street, Philadelphia.
E. W. Crichton, Oswego, Oregon.
A. G. Curtin, junior, Bellefonte, Centre county, Pa.
H. R. Curtin, Roland, Centre county, Pa.
Owen W. Davis, Bangor, Maine.
S. Eifurt, Riverton, Greenup county, Ky.

Samuel Erb, Lebanon, Pa

John M. Ferris, Wellsborough, Essex county, New York.

Henry A. Foster, Appleton, Wis.

J. C. Fuller, 1509 Spruce street, Philadelphia.

Charles H. Graves, Duluth, Minn.

Gardner Greene, Norwich, Conn.

E. R. Hall, Ispheming, Mich.

E. Hanson, Trenton, New Jersey.

William Hewitt, Trenton, New Jersey.

Joshua Hunsecker, Lenhartsville, Berks county, Pa.

D. S. Hunter, Shippensburg, Pa.

J. M. Kennedy, 218 South Fourth street, Philadelphia.

Theo. B. Klein, Palmyra, Lebanon county, Pa.

J. W. Lapsely, Shelby Iron Works, Ala.

Bernard Lauth, Howard, Centre county, Pa.

A. R. MacIntosh, Hanging Rock, Ohio.

Archibald McAllister, Royer, Blair county, Pa.

B. C. McManigal, Union Furnace, Hocking county, Ohio.

R. D. McManigal, Union Furnace, Hocking county, Ohio.

J. N. Meriam, Cambridgeport, Mass.

John Milnes, Shenandoah Iron Works, Page county, Va.

William Milnes, Jr., Shenandoah Iron Works, Page county, Va.

Hon. D. J. Morrell, Johnstown, Cambria county, Pa.

B. F. Morret, Douglassville, Berks county, Pa.

Belden Noble, 1423 I street, Washington, D. C.

Edward S. Noble, Elk Rapids, Antrim county, Mich.

H. H. Noble, Elk Rapids, Antrim county, Mich.

Samuel Noble, Anniston, Calhoun county, Ala.

W. C. Odiorne, Muirkirk, Prince George's county, Md.

E. M. Parrott, Greenwood Iron Works, Orange county, New York.

R. D. A. Parrott, Greenwood Iron Works, Orange county. New York.

E. Peckham, Kimmswick, Jefferson county, Mo.

H. S. Pickands, Bangor, Van Buren county, Mich.

Joseph D. Potts, 234 South Fourth street, Philadelphia.

W. M. Potts, Barnestown, Chester county, Pa.

John Royer, Royer, Blair county, Pa.

L. B. Seeley, corner Main and Fulsom street, San Francisco, Cal.

H. H. Seidel, 218 Pine street, Harrisburg, Pa.
J. A. Seidle, Marysville, Perry county, Pa.
H. D. Smith, Appleton, Wis.
F. R. Smucker, Williamsburg, Blair county, Pa.
S. R. Smucker, Williamsburg, Blair county, Pa.
J. K. Spang, Reading, Pa.
L. L. Springer, Chambersburg, Pa.
James M. Swank, 265 South Fourth street. Philadelphia.
Henry T. Townsend, 218 South Fourth street, Philadelphia.
Alfred L. Tyler, Anniston, Calhoun county, Ala.
George Valentine, Bellefonte, Centre county, Pa.
Robert Valentine, Bellefonte, Centre county, Pa.
Horace Ware, Columbia, Ala.
Hon. Willard Warner, Tecumseh, Cherokee county, Ala.
George B. Wiestling, Mont Alto, Franklin county, Pa.
William Wilhelm, Howard, Centre county, Pa.
E. B. Willard, Hanging Rock, Ohio.

AT the annual meeting of the Pennsylvania Board of Agriculture, held in Harrisburg, January 29, 1880, the following resolutions were adopted:

Resolved, That in the opinion of the members of this Board the present fence laws of Pennsylvania are relics of colonial times long since outgrown, and that we most respectfully but earnestly urge upon the Legislature at its next session, the necessity of making such changes in regard to fence laws as shall conform to the present conditions of agriculture in our State and the present needs and common law rights of farmers.

Resolved, That the executive committee be instructed to appoint such commission or commissions from the members of the Board as they may deem advisable to inquire into and report upon the undeveloped cleared pine lands and other resources of the State, as applied to agriculture.

A discussion upon the run-out fire, its purpose and economies, and a valuable contribution upon the Catalan forges of the country were promised, but were not received in time for this issue.

JUST as the JOURNAL goes to press we learn that the Spring Lake furnace, referred to on page 18, made 376 tons during its fifth week of blast. We expect to hear of it exceeding 400 tons per week.

JOURNAL

OF

UNITED STATES ASSOCIATION

OF

CHARCOAL IRON WORKERS.

EDITED BY THE SECRETARY.

No. 2. **AUGUST, 1880.**

Explanatory.

Some of the members of the association have expressed regret that No. 2 did not follow the initial number of the "Journal" at an earlier date. We prefer to advance rather than fall back, and, therefore, determined that in view of the expenses attending the organization of the association, and its presentation to those interested in the charcoal industry, that we would issue the Journal at such intervals as we could feel sure of maintaining. The purpose was to make these intervals three months, but personal affairs interposed at the allotted time, and caused additional delay.

We intend to keep the association out of debt, and therefore live within our exchequer. All the money expended has been devoted to our publication and to the interests of the association, no officer having received any salary from the funds in hand. The character, value, and interval of issue of the "Journal" will depend upon each individual iron-worker giving it his support, and we confidently expect that the second year of our existence as an association, will show such acquisitions to our membership as will permit us to promise the "Journal" at regular periods, and provide for more valuable articles.

We have so little literature on charcoal iron, that the preparation of items of interest, and the exertion to keep the "Journal" fresh and up with the times, requires more labor than is generally imagined. If each of our readers would forward data in his possession upon subjects treated of in these pages, and favor us with any points of interest pertaining to the operation of his own or neighboring works, records of fires, stoppage or renewing of operations at different charcoal industries, etc., the labor of preparation will be lightened and the character of the "Journal" improved.

Papers upon any matter of interest to the charcoal-iron industry will be acceptable; and we would urge the preparation of such for the annual meeting in October.

Without a systematic presentation of the "Journal" to manufacturers and others, we have been favored with a number of advertisements. Our desire is to make the "Journal" not only a record of matters of interest to the charcoal-iron trade, but also, by its advertisements, a directory telling where material and supplies can be obtained, and a medium through which managers, founders, forgemen, storekeepers, colliers, etc., can be secured, or find employment, and through which properties, woodland, wood or charcoal can be bought or offered for sale.

While our advertising pages are at the disposal of persons desiring to present anything required by the trade, we have no other space for sale, and any descriptions of works, processes, machinery, or apparatus which appear in the body of the "Journal," will be given because they may be considered of general interest to the constituency which our publication represents.

POROUS drain tile are now made of a mixture of saw-dust and plastic clay burned in ovens or kilns. The burning or charring of the small particles of wood form the pores in the otherwise compact mass of clay.

The Position of the Charcoal Iron Trade.

Mr. Swank has brought his annual reports as secretary of the American Iron and Steel Association to such perfection that they become encyclopædias of knowledge pertaining to the iron and steel industry; and their value is greatly enhanced by the reliability which is common to all statistical information emanating from his office.

The last report, dated May 20, 1880, contains so much of interest that we give place to some figures from it, which are arranged and amplified so as to be of most service to our readers.

Three millions seventy thousand eight hundred and seventy-five net tons is the amount of pig iron made in the United States in 1879. Of this 358,873 net tons were produced with charcoal, or less than 12 per cent. of the total out-put; yet this production of charcoal iron was only exceeded in the years 1856, and from 1868 to 1875 inclusive. As compared with the make of 1878, charcoal iron increased in greater proportion than that produced with either of the other fuels generally employed.

Mr. Swank gives the following production in net tons:

	Anthracite.	Bituminous.	Charcoal.	Total.
1878, ...	1,092,870	1,191,092	293,399	2,577,361
1879, ...	1,273,024	1,438,978	358,873	3,070,875
Increase, ...	180,154	247,886	65,474	493,514

The increase was, therefore, for all kinds of iron, 19.1 per cent.; for anthracite iron, 16.5 per cent; for bituminous iron, 20.8 per cent.; and for charcoal iron 22.3 per cent.

The charcoal pig iron made was divided up among the following States:

States.	Net tons in 1879.	Greatest Previous Production.	
		Year.	Net tons.
Michigan,	101,539	1874	128,969
Ohio,	43,445	1873	100,498
Pennsylvania,	35,895	1873	45,854
Alabama,	31,991	1874	32,863
Wisconsin,	31,430	1873	38,880
Maryland,	19,734	1873	30,315
New York,	18,129	1873	29,329
Missouri,	17,837	1874	49,093
Connecticut,	16,759	1873	26,977
Kentucky,	12,736	1873	42,219
Virginia,	7,703	1874	23,451
Tennessee,	7,567	1874	37,227
Massachusetts,	5,010	1874	17,777
Georgia,	4,133	1873	7,501
Oregon,	2,500	1874	2,500
Maine,	1,240	1876	3,002
Vermont,	625	1874	3,450
Texas,	400	1874	1,012
West Virginia,	200	1874	3,400
North Carolina,	None.	1873	1,432
Indiana,	None.	1874	2,100
Utah,	None.	1874	200
Totals,	358,873	1873	577,620

In the above table the maximum production of the various States and of the country, and date when same was made, from 1871 to present time, is given.

The only States which made less charcoal pig iron in 1879 than in 1878 were West Virginia, Kentucky, and Tennessee. Washington Territory, Minnesota, and California will be added to the list in 1880.

Over 28 per cent. of all the charcoal iron made in 1879 was produced in Michigan.

Of the 388 furnaces in blast in 1879, 103 were charcoal; and and of the 309 furnaces out of blast in 1879, 163 were charcoal.

To better illustrate the relative production of the various States from 1872 to 1879, we refer to the graphic representation which has been prepared for the "Journal," by C. Kirchkoff, Jr., M. E., Assistant Editor of the "Iron Age." The horizontal spaces designate years, and each division, on the vertical lines, represent 10,000 net tons.

To place the States in the table which did not produce 10,000

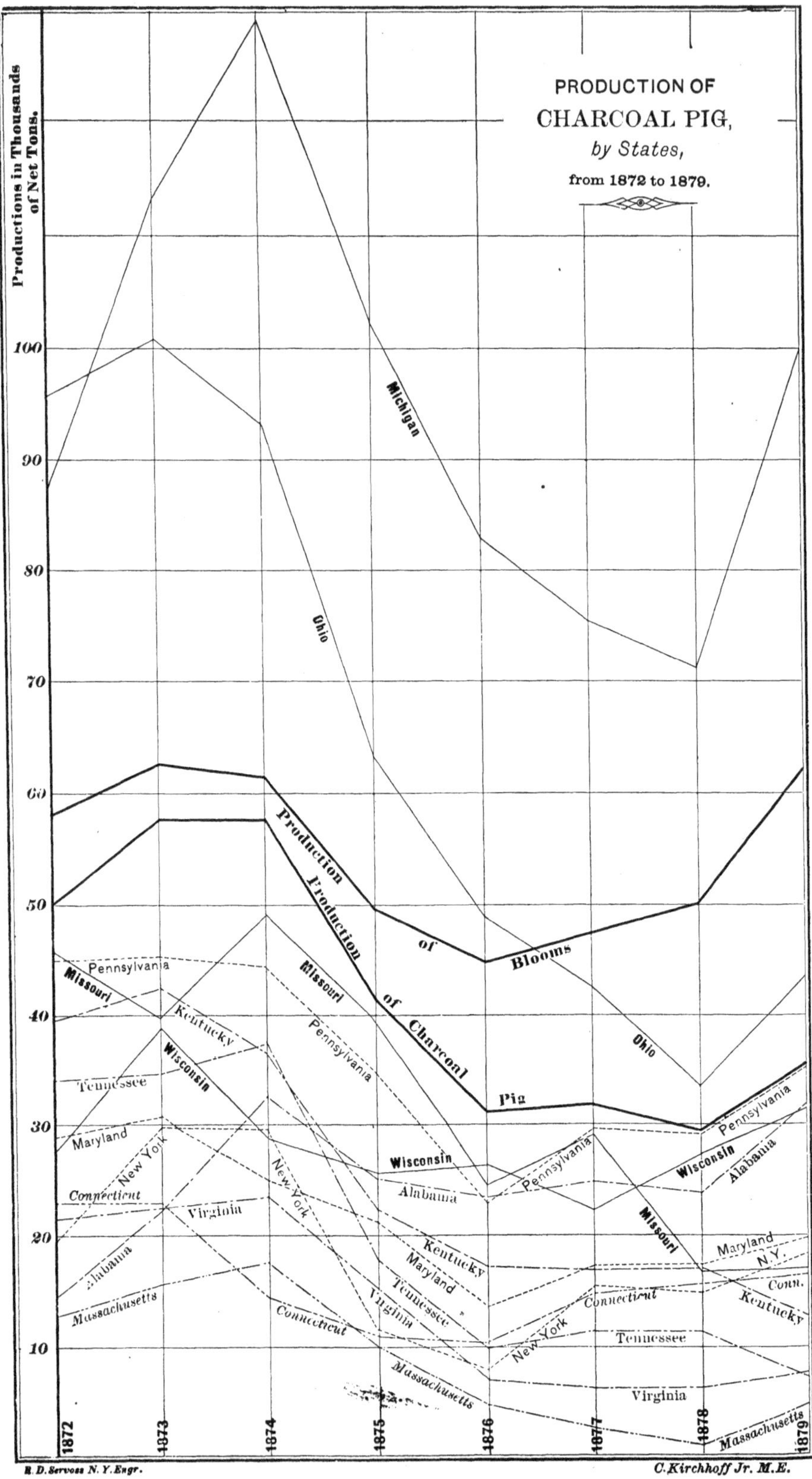
PRODUCTION OF
CHARCOAL PIG,
by States,
from 1872 to 1879.
Productions in Thousands of Net Tons.
100
90
80
70
60
50
40
30
20
10
Michigan
Ohio
Production of Blooms
Production of Charcoal Pig
Pennsylvania
Missouri
Kentucky
Wisconsin
Tennessee
Maryland
New York
Connecticut
Virginia
Alabama
Massachusetts
N.Y.
Conn.
1872
1873
1874
1875
1876
1877
1878
1879
R. D. Servoss N. Y. Engr.
C. Kirchhoff Jr. M.E.

tons or upwards, would have complicated the lines, but as it is, much of interest can be gained from a careful study of it. Mr. Kirchkoff writes in explanation:

"The diagram shows the fluctuations in the production of the various States which have, at any time, had an annual output exceeding 10,000 tons. It exhibits not alone the absolute quantities, but also the relative position of the various States, and the changes to which this position has been subject.

"For the sake of permitting an easy and ready comparison, we have given, also, a line for the total production of charcoal pig. As an attempt to add this on the same scale as the other data would carry the line far above the limits, we have assumed the scale to be ten times as large. One division, therefore, instead of representing 10,000 tons, gives 100,000. It will be noted, that, on the whole, the lines representing the production of the various States follow the general direction of that for the whole country. A feature which is quite strikingly exhibited, is, that the great western producers, Michigan and Ohio, are much more violent in their fluctuations than the trade in general. The numerous less important States, therefore, act favorably in steadying the total output. During the period from 1872 to 1879, both inclusive, Pennsylvania has quite well retained its position. Missouri, on the other hand, has exhibited some remarkable changes. Between 1872 and 1873, it has dropped off instead of gaining, as all the States, without an exception, had done. Both Kentucky and Tennessee are receding, while Wisconsin, Maryland, New York, and Connecticut have been holding their own. Alabama has been gaining in quite a considerable degree. From its position as thirteenth on the list in 1872, it is now the fourth, being smaller than Michigan, Ohio, and Pennsylvania only."

In 1879, 30,282 net tons of blooms and billets were made from ore, and 32,071 net tons were produced from pig and scrap iron, a total of 62,353 net tons, a quantity only exceeded since 1869 by the years 1871, when 63,000 net tons, and 1873, when 62,564 net tons were made. As compared with 1878, the production of blooms, &c., from ore, increased 25.4 per cent., and from pig and scrap, 23.8 per cent., an average increase from forges and blomaries combined of 24.5 per cent.

Of the 30,282 tons of blooms made in eight States from ore, 27,290 tons were produced in the State of New York, and the blomaries in Pennsylvania made 23,956 tons of blooms from pig iron and scrap; 8,115 tons being the production of all the other thirteen States having blomaries. Quite a large proportion of the New York ore blooms are consumed by the open-hearth steel works in producing superior steel plate, and many of the blooms are made and worked into billets before shipment.

The iron rolling-mills advanced their output in 1879 3.16 per cent. on the make of 1878, and the increase in production of all kinds of steel in 1879 exceeded by 27.7 per cent. that of 1878.

From these statements, it is evident, that although the charcoal iron industry represents but a small fraction in quantity of the iron trade of the country, it fairly kept pace in the improvement of trade.

As a large amount of the blooms made in forges, particularly those using pig iron, enters into the manufacture of plate iron, we have compared the production of blooms made from pig and scrap with that of plate and sheet iron since 1873:

Net Tons.	1873.	1874.	1875.	1876.	1877.	1878.	1879.
Charcoal blooms made in blomaries, . .	29,701	25,220	24,827	23,844	23,073	25,906	32,701
Plate and sheet iron, ...	169,169	176,888	192,769	165,255	182,242	182,042	269,768

In the published statistics, no separation of the plate and sheet iron is given. The blooms made from pig and scrap were not all used for plate iron, and many ore blooms were employed for this purpose, but the figures above given, will closely represent the quantity of charcoal blooms utilized by the plate iron mills.

Mr. Swank states, that the lowest price for Hanging Rock car wheel iron, at Cincinnati, was, in February, 1879, $28, and the highest was, in February, 1880, $63, and we might add, that blooms which sold at $50 in February, 1879, were purchased at $105 in February, 1880.

In the production of all kinds of pig iron, Pennsylvania stands first, making in 1870, 52⅓ per cent. of the total output; Ohio is second, New York third, and Michigan fourth, with New Jersey following closely.

Twenty-two States made pig iron in 1879, and twenty in 1878; the States of Indiana and Texas were the additions.

Four thousand two hundred and eighty miles of new railroad were built in 1879, increasing the mileage of the country to 86,121. The number of emigrants who came into the country during the year, was 250,565; both the miles of new railroad and number of emigrants will probably be greater in the present than in the past year.

In studying the figures and statistics given, we see much to encourage faith in continued business activity and in a ready market for a good quality of product.

There are, also, some interesting facts in the report concerning foreign iron producing countries, among which we mention the following:

In Prussia, there are 163 furnaces, 33 of which use charcoal for fuel; the product being largely run direct into castings.

In Austria and Hungary, there are 279 blast furnaces, over one half of which are run with charcoal.

Sweden has 366 charcoal furnaces, which produced in 1878, 372,000 net tons.

Spain, with an abundance of ore and forests, makes about as much charcoal pig iron as the State of Pennsylvania, and a considerable quantity of its wrought iron is produced in Catalan forges.

Switzerland has 3 charcoal furnaces and 1 coke furnace, also, a few charcoal forges.

Turkey has 127 Wolf furnaces for producing iron with charcoal, a most wasteful process; about 4,300 tons per annum being the total output.

Two hundred and eighty-four thousand one hundred and eleven tons of foreign ores, valued at $681,467 were imported during 1879, and the year 1880 will probably show over 300,000 tons of ore brought into the United States from other countries. About 60 per cent. of this ore is received at Philadelphia.

Forests of Washington Territory.

Mention was made on page 34, of No. 1 "Journal," of the valuable forests of north-west America, this has brought from Mr. Samuel Hadlock, of Port Townsend, pamphlets on North-western, Washington and the Puget Sound Iron Company, giving a description of five counties of that territory. From this we extract the following description of the forests, as of interest to our readers:

"The whole face of the country, with the exception of occasional prairies and marshes, is heavily timbered, principally with fir. In the lowlands is also found spruce, cedar, hemlock, soft maple, alder, etc., but the fir is the king of the forest, and, commercially, the most valuable. It grows tall, straight and large, and comparatively free from knots. Two hundred thousand feet is not an uncommon yield per acre, and, ordinarily, land that will yield less than 30,000 feet per acre is not now considered worth logging. Fir sticks of timber 150 feet long, 18×18 and even 24×24 inches, free from sap, crack or rent, and perfectly sound and straight, are not difficult to obtain. For ship building, Puget Sound fir has acquired a world-wide reputation, being equal to oak for strength and durability. It is equally adapted to house building and nearly all other purposes. It will hold a nail better than any other kind of wood, in fact the nail will generally break before it will draw out. There are about 20,000,000 acres of good timber land in the territory."

Apropos of what was said in reference to foreign exportation of lumber, we note that the amount exported from Puget Sound district fell from more than 41,000,000 to 25,000,000 feet last year, owing to the war between Peru and Chili; this is exclusive of spars, 2,000,000 pickets and 2,745,000 shingles. The Puget Sound Iron Company have now under contract a charcoal furnace, and in a short time we will have charcoal iron produced at the northeast, in Maine, in the northwest, at Puget Sound, in the extreme north, in Michigan, and in the far south, in Texas, besides that made in the works distributed throughout the more centrally located States.

Charcoal in the Patent Office.

In that great museum of American ingenuity, the Patent Office at Washington, there are on record, as models, drawings and specifications, something of interest to every known industry; and that branch in which we are particularly engaged is not without its representation in designs for machinery, fixtures, appliances and processes.

The manufacture of charcoal and the carbonization of wood has its fair share of patents, and they include quite a variety of topics, a brief summary of which we hope will prove interesting

There are several patents issued for peculiar methods of forming heaps or meilers, and quite a number covering peculiar shapes and construction of kilns. Among the latter is a semi portable kiln, consisting of an outer shell of wrought iron bolted together and lined with brick; another is a brick structure having a series of outside flues; a third is a kiln of brick with outside fire oven and draught-stack. There are several patents which were issued for kilns intended to be automatic in their action, by having a disk or plunger follow the decreasing bulk of the wood during its carbonization, and simultaneously closing the gas escape; one arrangement of similar purpose is a kiln with a telescopic inverted tank, acting like a gas holder, and following the shrinkage in volume as the process is advanced.

There are quite a number of patented kilns arranged to collect more or less of the by-products of distillation, some are encircled by pipes, and some carbonize the wood on cars which are run into kilns or large metallic retorts; others are constructed to have the wood carbonized by pipes heated by air, gases, or by superheated steam, and one patent provides a means of utilizing the acetic vapors from wood carbonization, by exhausting them from the kiln by a fan and forcing them through the requisite distilling apparatus.

The inventions embracing form and arrangement of retorts for charring wood, and for the connected apparatus for collecting the products are quite numerous, some of them being complex and others rather crude, any attempt at description of which, unless in detail, would be unsatisfactory. Judging by the record of the Patent Office, considerable attention has been given to the distillation of pine wood and production of tar, turpentine, etc.

Among the patents for producing charcoal is a horizontal retort, containing a revolving cage charged with wood for the purpose of producing "charbon roux;" another is for a horizontal cylindrical retort with a flue passing through the center, to obtain thorough charring for gunpowder charcoal; another is a retort, crescent shape, in cross section so as to give approximately equal thickness of material for carbonization, set on an incline to decrease the labor of charging and discharging.

There are about forty United States patents relating to wood carbonization, a majority of which provide for the utilization of the resulting acetic vapors and tar; an evidence of the appreciation of the importance of preventing the great waste arising from the production of most of our charcoal. We hope at another time to take up this subject of patents more in detail, and trace out what has been done in the utilization of the by-products of carbonization and the results attained.

The Muirkirk Furnace.

Many of our readers will be surprised to know that within fourteen miles of the capital of the country there is a charcoal furnace in active operation and doing very good work. This plant is known as the Muirkirk furnace, and is located on the Washington city branch of the Baltimore and Ohio railroad. It was erected in 1847, and was in constant operation from 1860 to 1874; idle during part of the panic, but now averaging about fifty-five tons of car-wheel iron, under the personal management of Mr. Charles E. Coffin, proprietor, to whom we are indebted for the illustration which we publish. In the view, the observer is looking towards Washington, D. C.

The stack is built of brick, the lower portion being square, with openings forming three tuyere arches and a fore-arch. The upper portion is cupola shaped, banded. The bosh is 100 inches in diameter, and the total height is 29 feet. The crucible is 50 inches in diameter and 42 inches high. It is pierced by three tuyeres projecting 4 inches into the crucible at a height of 30 inches.

Blast is supplied by a vertical steam engine, 24 inches by 36 inches, blowing through three $2\frac{3}{4}$ to $3\frac{1}{2}$ nozzles, at a pressure of about 1 pound.

The boshes are quite steep, extending 10 feet above the bottom, and then running vertically for 2 feet more.

From here the inwalls slope to the throat, which is 4 feet 3 inches diameter, fitted with a 30-inch bonnet extending 4 feet down into the furnace.

The crucible and bosh walls are but 16 inches thick, made of fire-clay blocks and secured by bands.

The furnace is worked open top, with closed front and Lurman cinder notch. The blast is heated in a hot oven, consisting of 18 cast-iron pipes of ∞ cross-section, and steam is generated in a boiler 48 diameter and 26 feet long, with two flues 17 inches diameter. The iron is made from local ores, averaging in the furnace 38 per cent., having been first calcined in appropriate kilns.

The fuel is obtained from the country adjacent, and is made from oak, chestnut, and pine, the latter predominating. Oyster shells are used for flux, principally hauled one mile by teams, but some are brought to the furnace by railroad.

Tests of the pig iron have been made and 10 samples of No. 4 pig averaged over 41,000 pounds tensile strength per square inch. The iron is used to make cannon for the Government, the celebrated 40 ton gun, tested a year or so ago at Sandy Hook, having been made largely of it.

We shall be pleased to publish similar descriptions of other furnaces or forges, if our friends will send the details. An illustration of the works always adds interest, as it not only shows the disposition of the various parts of the plant, but gives an idea of the location and surroundings.

The notes for this sketch were made during the very pleasant meeting of the executive committee of the association at Muirkirk, when we did our best to increase the stock of flux for the furnace.

A Bushel of Charcoal, II, (by Weight.)

Although most of our charcoal iron works use the bushel of a specified number of cubic inches capacity, the variations in standard of which were given in No. 1 Journal, pages 27 to 31, a fair proportion employ a standard of weight in fixing the bushel, and the transportation of charcoal by railroads, which is yearly growing in favor, has undoubtedly done much to increase the number of iron works who use the weight standard.

There is as much uncertainty about what a bushel of charcoal is in pounds, as in cubic inches; we have records extending all the way from 11 pounds to $22\frac{4}{10}$ pounds. Undoubtedly, the established avoirdupois of a bushel of charcoal, originally came from the actual weight of a specified quantity, but as different methods of charring and kinds of wood produce charcoal of varying specific gravities, the custom in certain localities was probably determined by these causes. The bushel, by weight, has been *growing*, for one manager could not afford to pay as much for 18 pounds of charcoal, as his neighbor who received 20 pounds for his bushel; then 20 pounds was a convenient standard, for 100 bushels weighed a net ton; but as 2,240 is also a ton by our peculiar laws, 22.4 pounds came to be used as a bushel, because 100 of these also weigh a ton. A fair average of the bushels by weight used throughout the country, may be set down as 20 pounds.

Svedelius, in his hand-book for charcoal burners, prepared for the Swedish Government, says:

"Fresh charcoal, also re-heated charcoal, contains scarcely any water, but when cooled, it absorbs it very rapidly, so that after twenty-four hours, it may contain 4 to 8 per cent. of water. After the lapse of a few weeks, the moisture of charcoal may not increase perceptibly, and may be estimated at 10 to 15 per cent., or an average of 12 per cent.* That charcoal made from more solid kinds of wood absorbs less water, while porous, partially dried charcoal, absorbs more, needs no explanation.

"Black, solid, and perfectly good charcoal is indeed heavier than that which is loose and porous, but, on the other hand, it is lighter than that which has not been thoroughly charred. Regardless of the moisture and the manner of charring, the charcoal of some kinds of wood is, of itself, considerably heavier than that made of other kinds; charcoal made from foliferous trees is usually heavier and more solid than that made from coniferous trees. Young trees produce lighter charcoal than older ones.

"In determining the quality of charcoal, then it is necessary both to see and weigh it, and it is perfectly natural that the figures given to represent the weight of charcoal differ very much. As a general rule, we may assume that a cubic foot of charcoal carefully made from well seasoned pine, weighs about 9 pounds, and a cubic foot made from spruce, 8 pounds."

We have often been asked the question: "What is the proper weight for a bushel of charcoal?" We could make a partially satisfactory answer if we had a uniform bushel by measure to go by.

In Percy's Metallurgy, there appears the following table, show-

---

*** A thoroughly charred piece of charcoal ought, then, to contain about 84 parts carbon, 12 parts water, 3 parts ash, and 1 part hydrogen.**

ing the weight of a cubic meter or stere of charcoal from different woods in the French Pyrenees. We have reduced the quantities to pounds per cubic foot, and placed them in parallel column with Percy's data:

	Kilogrammes per cubic meter.	Pounds per cubic foot.
Black oak, twenty-five years old,	235	14.7
Beech, coppice wood, nineteen years old,	229	14.3
Beech, large,	218	13.6
Chestnut, young,	192	12
Scotch fir, branches,	173	10.8
Silver fir, large wood and branches,	152	9.5
Alder,	141	8.8

The same authority states, that a cubic meter of charcoal made in circular piles in France from a mixture of hard and soft woods, weighed from 220 to 180 kilogrammes, or from 13.7 to 11.2 pounds per cubic foot.

To adopt a standard for calculation, we will take the United States bushel of 2,150.42 cubic inches of distilled water, and add cone 6 inches high=2,748 cubic inches, or 1.59 cubic feet. Therefore, by multiplying the above weight by 1.59, we have the weight of a bushel of 2,748 cubic inches, which varies from 14 pounds for the alder, to 23.5 pounds for black oak. The average of pit coal made of mixed woods as above being 20 pounds.

In Prussian iron works, a cubic foot of charcoal made from Scotch fir weighed from 10.3 to 10.6 pounds, and made from oak or beech from 13.2 to 14.1 pounds; these figures closely harmonize with those given in the table.

The following quotation is from Flower's "History of Tin and Tin Plates:"

"The usual Welsh mode of selling charcoal, is by the dozen tubs, each measuring 36×36×20 inches, about 15 cubic feet, and weighing roughly about a ton. When charcoal is bought by measurement in the woods, the charcoal burner is privileged to measure one of his legs in the tub."

As a dozen of these tubs contain 180 cubic feet, and weigh 1 ton, a bushel of 2,748 cubic inches would weigh 20 pounds.

We have made some personal investigations which partially verify the foreign data given, but they are not extended enough to form any fair conclusions.

While operating the Fletcherville furnace, in Essex county, New York, Mr. T. F. Witherbee coaled in a 60-cord kiln, various woods separately, and obtained the following weights per bushel of 2,688 inches:

Birch, ...	17.025	lbs.	Hemlock, ...	12.85	lbs.
Black Ash, . . .	14.475	"	Basswood, . . .	10.625	"
Poplar, ...	12.275	"	White Pine, . . .	9.8	"
White Ash, . . .	16.325	"	Spruce, ...	11.25	"
Maple, ...	18.95	"	Yellow Birch, . .	18.75	"

As this coal was weighed while the kilns were being emptied, and before there was an opportunity to absorb moisture, an allowance of 12 per cent. should be made. This would make the average bushel of 2,748 cubic inches weigh about 17 pounds, considerably less than that noted above.

The equalization of weight and measure is important to all in the charcoal-iron trade, and if the facts are given we shall be glad to work out and publish such a tabulated statement, as will permit each to intelligently compare his working with that of other similar industries. We shall, therefore, be thankful if our readers will each, as far as he has facilities, obtain accurate weights of given volumes of various characters of charcoal and forward to the secretary. All that is required is to give the *exact* dimensions of the barrow, wagon, or other receptacle, its correct gross weight "even full" of charcoal, and the actual weight of the receptacle, together with a memorandum of the proportions of different kinds of wood from which the coal is made, and if possible the age of the wood, and whether the coal is fresh or from stock.

Such a table is needed and we would urge coöperation upon all our friends.

Having now considered a bushel by measure and a bushel by weight, we have to examine into the relative advantages of each.

In purchasing coal or paying colliers for their work, the benfits of using a measure of capacity are—

1st. Brands and dirt, particularly from pit coal, which weigh more than charcoal for same bulk, (some of which will be received in spite of rigid supervision,) are only paid for at same rate as charcoal, while if measured by weight an additional price is paid for this less valuable material.

2d. No water is paid for. Berzelius states that he found the ordinary run of charcoal 24 hours old to contain from 10 to 12 per cent. of water absorbed from the atmosphere. Percy gives three analyses by Faisst, showing respectfully 6.04, 7.23, 8.21 per cent. of moisture in fresh charcoal.

The natural absorption of moisture is often supplemented by water thrown on the charcoal by teamsters to extinguish fires, or to add to its weight; or in quenching kilns.

3d. Transportation reduces the volume more rapidly than the weight of charcoal, and, therefore, a wagon which, at the coaling, was loaded with a given number of bushels upon a standard of equalized volume and weight, would contain a less number of bushels on arrival at destination, if measured, than if weighed.

4th. The mud on wagons, snow on car-roofs, or other outside weight, need not be considered, and the system of dockage necessitated by these matters is not required.

On the other hand the advantages of using a standard of weight are—

1st. Soft and bulky coal, being light, is not paid for at the same rate as hard and compact coals, but in purchasing or contracting by a weighed bushel, the iron master pays practically by the pound of carbon, and a hard dense fuel especially advantageous for blast furnace use is more likely to be obtained.

2d. In charging fuel to forge fires or blast furnaces a regularity can be secured with weighed coal, generally impracticable with measured coal, therefore the consumption of fuel per ton of metal can be kept at a lower amount, and the operation of the works maintained more reliably and satisfactorily.

3d. If kilns convenient to the furnace are employed, there being no dirt or outside weights to allow for, the coal if weighed secures the fairest method of making a standard, both for settlement and for charging, for the denser the coal, if well made, the more weight has been handled in filling the kiln.

We consider that the most satisfactory method is to deliver the charcoal on the furnace bank or into stock-houses by measure, and to charge it into furnace or forge fire by weight. This obviates paying for dirt, dust, brands, water, etc., and also does away largely with dockage. The coal on bank or in stock having about a uniform amount of moisture absorbed, the charges contain carbon proportionate to their weight, and therefore a more intelligent management of the plant is possible, than where the quantity of carbon is a matter of supposition only, based on a general average.

The occasional comparison of a few loads will give data for establishing equalized measures by weight and volume, the former having margin sufficient to cover loss in handling.

We incline to the opinion that the weighed bushel will continue to grow in favor, for as the use of kilns and retorts becomes more general, the advantages of employing the measured bushel are less apparent. The abandonment of meiler charring, which to a great extent is inevitable as our wooded areas decrease, and the necessity of economizing is forced upon us, will place the coaling under closer supervision of the manager, and the product being free from dirt, and charged fresh, will be most satisfactorily used by the weight standard.

Dr. P. G. Snyder, Superintendent of Ellendale forge, Dauphin county, Pennsylvania, has patented a vertical forge hammer, designed to be operated by a water wheel or steam engine. The power is applied by belt to a pulley on a horizontal shaft which also carries a fly-wheel and a cam. By the revolution of the cam it strikes a projection on the hammer-rod, thus raising the rod and the bit connected to it. When the cam has passed the projection the ram falls on the anvil-block below, or upon anything placed upon it for manipulation. A frame work or housings of iron, which carries all the working parts, extend from the bed-plate and form guides for the hammer-rod to work in.

2

Iron Works of Great Britain.

A map of the iron works, iron ore mines, and coal districts of Great Britain, on a scale of about 25 miles per square inch, has been published by "Ryland's Iron Trade Circular," of Birmingham, England, which is of particular interest, as showing the distribution of the iron works and the various centers of pig iron production. By an examination of it we find that a parallelogram measuring 350 miles north and south, by 175 miles east and west, will include every iron works and most of the ore and coal deposits; and with one or two exceptions, every iron works in the kingdom would be found in a circle described, with a radius of 170 miles from Preston as a center. When we consider that in this limited area, which is further reduced when the water space is deducted, there are congregated 948 blast furnaces, and numerous mills, mines, etc., while the 697 blast furnaces in the United States are scattered through 26 States and Territories, we can form more comprehensive ideas as to this industry in the two nations.

The following table shows the number of furnaces built, and the number in blast at last report, in the different portions of England and in Scotland and Wales:

	Number of furnaces.	Number in blast.
Cumberland,	53	44
Derbyshire,	55	41
Durham,	61	23
Lincolnshire,	18	16
Lancashire,	51	40
Northamptonshire,	23	17
Staffordshire,	182	90
Shropshire,	25	12
Yorkshire,	148	113
Scattering,	22	8
Total in England,	638	404
Total in Wales,	159	78
Total in Scotland,	151	117
Grand totals,	948	599

Tin-Plate.

There is probably no single industry the encouragement of which would do more to create a demand for the higher grades of charcoal irons than the manufacture of tin-plates; but although there are two works now in existence in this country, and our annual consumption would keep fifty such works in operation, there is not a pound of tin-plate now produced in the United States.

This state of affairs was brought about by the Treasury Department expunging from the tariff laws a comma, which makes the law so read that the duty on tin-plate instead of being $2\frac{1}{2}$ cents per pound is but $1\frac{1}{10}$ cents per pound, the duty being less on tin-plates than on the iron from which it is made. Galvanized iron pays $2\frac{1}{2}$ cents per pound, cold rolled sheet-iron 3 cents.

To manufacture the 2,000,000 boxes of tin annually imported into this country will consume 150,000 tons of pig iron, of which fully one third would be made from charcoal pig iron, one third bloomed with charcoal from scrap, and one third produced with coke or anthracite irons.

In a late English publication entitled "History of Tin and Tin-plate," by Phillip William Flower, there are some very interesting facts pertaining to the iron industry and illustrations of ancient processes. We have made a number of extracts from this work and present them for our readers. In the quotations we have not used asterisks to designate matter eliminated, and in a few instances we have changed phraseology where it was necessary to combine sentences; but in no case has the intention of the author been misconstrued by altering the sense of his writings, which evidence intelligent investigation and patient research. The quotations from the book are so marked, and are as near verbatim as our limited space would permit.

"Used as a coating for iron in the manufacture of tin-plates, tin finds its largest and most expanding market. Tin of itself would bruise, would bend, would melt, and moreover would prove far too valuable for the thousand and one purposes for which tin-plates are employed. It is, then, the skillful combination of tin and iron which has created the immense and ever-increasing consumption.

"Tin-plate, or in other words, tinned plate, or, as the French people call it, "white iron," is a material which, in a converted shape, is familiar to everybody under the name of tin, but few, indeed, of the world are aware that their so-called "block tin" tea-pot, kettle, or dish-cover, is made of nine parts iron, and one part tin."

The manufacture of this material was first established in Bohemia, being in existence there prior to 1600. It was first successfully carried on in France in 1714; in England in 1720 to 1725; and introduced into Sweden in 1739.

"Tin plates vary in size, in substance, in toughness, and in the nature of their coating. In sizes, from a sheet of 10 × 14 inches to a sheet of 40 × 28. In substance, from a sheet of taggers, as thin as paper itself, to a plate of ten times that thickness, adapted for the dish-covers of ordinary use; in toughness, from a sheet which won't bend at all, to a sheet of charcoal-iron, which is equal in tenacity to leather itself. The lightest coating is sufficient for mustard and biscuit purposes; the heaviest possible coating is desired for dish-covers, which have to stand planishing in conversion, and will be subsequently subject to the inevitable ceaseless 'rubbing' in every careful household."

"Tin-plates of commerce are bought and sold under the general term of 'coke' or 'charcoal,' this distinction relating, of course, to the nature of the iron from which the plates were made."

The covering or plating affects the title as tin or terne-plates, the latter being dipped in a mixture of tin and lead.

"Iron well made in the forge cannot be materially affected, either for better or worse, by any subsequent process of manufacture, and on the other hand, iron poorly made cannot, by all the care in the world, be improved upon after it has taken the shape of bar iron."

The quality of the iron employed, therefore, determines the character of the "tin plate;" the best grade is produced from charcoal pig, manipulated in charcoal fires.

In reference to forgemen, the author says:

"The hours of work are from 6, A. M., to 6, P. M., or *vice versa*, or until the hour within that time when the proper number of "rounds" has been completed; generally the turns are changed at the times above mentioned, when it is etiquette for the men who are leaving work to put everything about the fires ready, in good order for the men who will arrive."

This is more sensible than spoiling both day and night by changing turn at unseasonable hours, as is the custom largely in the United States.

"All forge work is paid for by weight. The materials are weighed in, and the result is weighed out at the beginning and end of each turn. As a rule, a finer or hammerman can earn ten shillings for a day of ten hours, during which he only attends to his fire and to the manipulation under the hammer, all fetching or carrying being done for him by laborers or coachers.

"The helve is the oldest and at the same time the best known means of forging out iron. It is suitable for steam or water power. It consists of a heavy piece of cast iron which is lifted by a cam and falls by its own weight upon the iron which it is required to forge. There is no coaxing or nursing with this kind of a hammer. It must be good iron, or it will splash all to pieces, and it is sure to be well hammered, for the blow regulates itself.

"In former times, the head of the helve was raised by the pressure of a cam coming downwards upon the tail, now it is always usual to raise the head by the upward movement of the cam; but it does not matter very much how this operation is performed, so long as the hammer does fall, the result upon the iron is the same."

From the description, we presume the hammer ordinarily employed, is one familiar in this country, the bit, helve, and husk or journals being cast in one piece.

"Until the latter part of the seventeenth century, all the tin produced in Cornwall, whether from streams or mines, was smelted in blast furnaces with charcoal. The first air furnace for smelting tin was erected about the year 1680, since that period nearly all the mine tin of Cornwall has been smelted in air furnaces."

All tin used in Great Britain has been obtained from Cornwall, some of the mines extending out under the sea, but the expense of procuring it, has brought into competition with the home product the tin from the East Indies and Australia. The ores are known as "stream tin" and "mine tin," the former being washed, the latter mined, stamped, and separated. The "stream tin" is superior, and it is mostly smelted in blast furnaces, the product being called "grain tin," which is employed by dyers and for the finer processes. The "mine tin" is principally smelted in reverberatory furnaces with coke, and the product is known as "block tin."

In his remarks on charcoal, Mr. Flower excites our interest by statements which point to the supposition that the utilization of the acetic vapors is not neglected in Great Britain, and in his reference to the permanence of the charcoal supply and the carriage of wood, the latter being a universal bugbear among Americans. One of the topics which we expect to discuss shortly in the "Journal," is the transportation of charcoal, the possible economies of carrying wood to convenient kilns from various distances, and the extent to which the superior yield possible in kilns, counterbalances the cost of bringing wood to them.

"Charcoal was at one time the refuse of a manufacture which was carried on for the production of naptha and sugar of lead; now the value of charcoal has been cleverly forced to such a point, that it is said the chemicals are the refuse of the charcoal, which ranges in value from 30s. to 60s. per ton, and has been recently selling for a much higher price."

The rate here given is equivalent to from 6 to 12 cents per bushel of 20 pounds.

"It might be supposed, that after all these years of iron manufacture, there would have been great difficulty in obtaining fuel for the purpose; but this, in fact, is not the case, for there is always plenty of charcoal "offering," and it is not unusual for quantities of 1,000 tons to be bought and sold in one bargain."

"Formerly, all the charcoal was burnt in the woods, and was carried in sacks by mules to its destination. This was all very well so long as there was plenty of wood to be found in the immediate neighborhood. Now the bulk of the charcoal is made at a charcoal works from wood which is brought from long distances by sea and rail."

"The Boom," and What it Cost.

When our first number of the "Journal" was issued the iron trade was, to use a popular expression, "booming," within a fortnight after the "Journal" had reached its readers the "boom" had become a matter of history, and the rapidly declining prices caused many to hesitate in re-building old or projecting new iron works. Up to within a short time the trade has had a continuous downward tendency, and as a consequence, there has been a number of serious commercial failures.

We, however, see no reason for despondency, for the depression was not due to a panic, nor to a decreased consumption, but resulted from an overstocked market.

During the long-continued business inactivity, the consumers of the product of our iron works, being scant of orders, made few purchases, and carried extremely light stocks. Car wheels, rails and machinery were kept in use for economy sake when new ones should have been substituted. As the revival of business gradually developed, the demand for pig and manufactured iron was increased, and prices were stiffened; then consumers, hastening to stock-up, sent the quotations to a higher figure, until the market assumed such a character as to encourage heavy speculation and large importations of foreign iron. The natural sequence of such a course was a sudden collapse of the bubble so highly inflated, and an apparently serious blow to our great iron industry.

To appreciate to what extent our trade has been influenced by foreign importations, we have the figures prepared by the American Iron and Steel Association, showing that from December 1st, 1879, to July 1st, 1880, the following amounts of pig iron, manufactured iron, and steel were imported into the country from England alone:

Pig iron,	539,250
Bar iron,	50,480
Railroad iron,	135,154

Hoops, sheets and plates,	34,990
Tin-plate,	97,067
Cast or wrought iron,	4,844
Old iron, principally rails,	223,487
Steel,	32,267
Total gross tons,	1,117,539

While these quantities are startling in their tabulated form, they are more so when compared with our iron-producing capacity.

By reducing the manufactured irons and steel to pig iron, that is, by taking the number of tons of pig iron necessary to produce these quantities, we find that in the 7 months a total of 1,210,000 gross tons of pig iron of British manufacture were utilized for American consumption. This is equal to the practical out-put for the same time of 48 per cent. of all the furnaces of this country, or an amount as great as could be produced in 2½ months, if it were possible for every furnace in the land to be in operation simultaneously, and working to its full published capacity. To make this quantity of pig iron would occupy the entire active capacity of our charcoal furnaces nearly two years, or, if every charcoal furnace were worked to its utmost continuously for 17 months, no more iron would be produced than was imported into this country from England in 7 months. And to turn out blooms sufficient to make the amount of hoop, sheet and plate iron imported in the 7 months, would have necessitated the continuous operation of every forge and bloomary to its full extent for a period of 13 weeks.

If to this we add the tin-plate imported, we have the surprising exhibit that enough manufactured iron for hoops, plates, sheets, and tin-plate came into the country from England in 7 months to keep every forge and bloomary busy for a year. Undoubtedly, much of the material was not made of as high a grade as charcoal blooms, but we anticipate that enough blooms would be used for manufacturing the amount of steel to make up any deficiency.

But other countries besides England sought a market here, and it is probable that during these seven months the United States has consumed 1,400,000 gross tons of foreign pig-iron.

With such an addition to our own out-put, is it remarkable that there has been a collapse, and is it surprising that, with an importation of about one half the active capacity of our furnaces for 7 months, we had no consumption to meet it?

Foreign irons are still being received on previous contracts, but in gradually diminishing quantities; and the additional European iron-works started up with the profits from what was sent to our market, menace with their increasing stocks any immediate great improvement in prices.

There has been a serious decline in the prices of charcoal irons, but it has been slower, and they have suffered less severely than others, although there was of necessity considerable sympathy with the balance of the iron trade. This was owing to three causes:

1st. As most of the product of charcoal iron-works is employed for special purposes on account of superior quality, and the production of it is limited, the demand continued more uniform.

2d. The decline came at a most opportune time for charcoal furnaces. Many had used up their stock of charcoal and had blown out, or were about doing so. New furnaces starting up or being repaired could not depend on a supply of fuel until the season was further advanced, and stocks in hand were light.

3d. Much of the iron imported was of an inferior quality, and better grades were of necessity used to make it *passably good.* We will yet hear of damaging results from the use of so much inferior material for structural purposes.

By the existence of the first of these causes, we are strengthened in the belief which was proclaimed in the former issue of the Journal, and which we shall continue to express, that *the success and permanence of the charcoal iron industry is dependent upon the manufacture of strictly quality iron.* We have visited a number of our charcoal iron works, but have yet to see one which could afford to make poor iron.

In moving the immense block of foreign iron into this country, we not only lost the sale of that quantity of our own product, but paid for much of it at higher figures than the average of our own furnaces received, for many iron works here had sold largely in advance, and but a few obtained any appreciable advantage from the extreme high prices.

Thanks to the protection given by the Government, we feel that trade will grow better in the future rather than decline. The American demand stimulated trade in England to such an extent that 142 additional furnaces were blown in; and these have been accumulating stock, standing ready to again supply our market, if it were not for the tariff which the Government imposes on foreign iron.

We have abiding faith in our own resources and capacity of consumption, and believe that home business interests can utilize every ton of pig iron which our well-located furnaces can manufacture; but we cannot care for the product of foreign nations, or of home plants so poorly situated, equipped, or managed that iron can only be made at a profit when the price is far above its intrinsic value; for iron undoubtedly has an intrinsic value as well as gold or silver, and any advance beyond this forces iron, ores, labor, and supplies to false values from which sooner or later they must recede with disastrous results.

Who can truly estimate what the "boom" cost us? The profit lost on nearly one and a half million tons of pig, and the manufactured iron and steel, does not represent it. The many millions of days' labor in extracting ores, producing fuels, operating furnaces, puddling, sinking, heating, rolling, or converting, and the tonnage on our own railroads of the stock to make the material, the material itself and the supplies required, demonstrate that the loss extended into every branch of trade.

The shock resulting from the sudden fall in prices staggered all business, but we see about us encouraging signs for a healthy revival, and fair remunerative prices for iron. Let us prepare ourselves to share in its advantages, by perfecting our works and processes so as to manufacture in the most economical manner a product whose superiority will command the highest market rates.

We believe that prices will be maintained, and that business will daily grow better, being necessarily affected by the uncertainties attending the season of national political excitement, but we expect no "boom." The iron trade wants no sudden inflation to encourage the existence of industries which can only live at such times, and as soon as a revulsion comes, bring distrust by financial disaster.

The iron trade will thrive best when economies of operation and quality of product are most studied. Cheap manufacture, not high prices, will add most to the success of the industry.

The "Run-out" Fire.

Most of the forges using pig iron for making blooms, employ an intermediate process familiarly known as the "run-out fire," wherein the pig iron is refined, and a portion of its impurities removed. Quite a number of forges work raw pig, that is, pig iron is charged directly into the forge fires.

The advantages of the run-out or finery fire, consist in its purifying or refining character, and also the possibility of obtaining a more uniform metal than is possible when *raw pig* is used, but it is an expensive process, and as usually employed, requires an expenditure of from one eighth to one fifth the price of the bloom.

The forge fires working raw pig, require more coal than those using metal previously refined, because the work done in the run-out must, in this case, be performed in the forge fires at a consequent increased consumption of fuel. But in the use of raw pig, all grades of iron cannot be satisfactorily employed, and to get good results, a sharp or low grade pig iron, ordinarily made with cold blast, is employed, which necessitates keeping the furnace working so cold as to subject it to every change of temperature or of stock. White and grey irons are often mixed, more, however, with a view of utilizing the stock on hand than from choice, for a close iron approaching "mottled" in grade, is generally preferred.

As to the mere matter of cost, we incline in favor of the blooms made from raw pig, for the labor, fuel, and maintenance at the run-out fire undoubtedly amount to more than the excess of fuel and labor required by the pig metal in the forge fire. But where a furnace and forge are worked by the same party, it is more than probable that the regularity of product secured by the use of the run-out fire, and the convenient utilization of the entire out-put of the furnace, will make blooms at but little if any advance over that of those from raw pig, and the product will average better.

From the records examined, we find the loss of metal from pig iron to blooms is, in either case, about equal. One series of experiments to which we have had access, show that 1,000 pounds of hot blast charcoal iron run out and then worked in forge fires, yielded on an average of 756.13 pounds of blooms, and 1,000 pounds of cold blast pig iron worked "raw" in the forge fires, produced an average of 723.55 pounds of blooms.

Twenty-four gross tons of pig iron were used in these experiments, and the consumption of charcoal in forge fires was in the proportion of 10 bushels with run-out metal, to 11 bushels with cold blast metal.

Such being the case, the run-out fire may be considered as an advantage, and our object should be to so reduce its cost, as to bring it under the claim of superiority on account of cost as well as quality.

In two instances, of which we have knowledge, an attempt has been made to economize, by allowing the refined metal to flow directly from the run-out fire into the forge fires. This has been tried by the Trenton Iron Company, at Trenton, New Jersey, and is at present done at Cove forge, at Williamsburg, Blair county, Pennsylvania.

The principal objection we see to this process is, that it requires a duplication of finery fires, otherwise the forge fires all receive their charges too near together to secure proper working and rotation in the use of the hammer. But this might be overcome with a forge having, say 10 or 12 fires, using two run-out fires which tap the metal directly into ladles, by which it is carried to the various fires.

A mass of metal sufficient to charge five or six fires should retain its heat long enough to give ample intervals in supplying them. It is done every day in foundries.

That the hot run-out is economical would seem obvious, for a considerable quantity of fuel is, of course, saved in the forge fires, and we can see no reason why it should be at all disadvantageous in affecting the quality of the product, unless, as we have seen, the cinder does not separate so thoroughly as when cold.

Continuous processes are being generally introduced into the manufacture of iron, and there appears to be no good reason why they should not work advantageously in the production of blooms. In fact, economical results would seem to be best obtained by not allowing any more heat to be lost than is absolutely necessary, and our ideal of a charcoal forge, is an arrangement where the pig iron and cinder or ore are heated by the fuel from a previous charge, and when the metal is refined, it is run hot in the forge fires. The hot bloom or slab being taken from the hammer direct to a heating furnace and there subjected to a "wash heat," then passed through breaking down rolls, and converted into billets, covers, or other rough shapes for the final processes in the mills.

We have considered the various phases of such processes, and see no cause to doubt their practicability. We cannot expect successful issue to every experiment, but we believe a plant arranged as described will work advantageously and permit of producing billets or covers at an expense no greater than the cost of blooms or slabs as ordinarily made. The inquiry naturally follows, why not go further and tap from blast furnace into run-out fires. It is possible that this too might be accomplished, but to do this, the furnace must be opened at such times as the run-out fire is ready to be charged. The run-out and forge fires are, therefore, directly dependent upon getting their work out upon the operation or delays at the furnace. The cinder for run out would have to be previously heated, and at least part of the iron must be run into pigs in any event.

As to the purifying effect of the run-out, the following partial analyses of ores, pig iron, run out metal, run-out cinder, blooms, and forge cinder are presented. The ore averaged 48 per cent. of iron in the furnace.

	Pig iron.	Run-out metal.	Run-out cinder.	Forge cinder.	Ore.
Silicon, ...	1.019	0.208			
Sulphur, ...	None.	0.015	0.140	. . . . .	None.
Phosphorus, ...	0.251	0.090	0.777	0.351	0.12
Silica, ...	. . . . .	. . . . .	15.410	5.530	

The ore had a tendency to be cold short, but the coke used in the run-out fire parted with some of its sulphur, which passed into the run-out metal from which a neutral bloom was made.

Eighty per cent. of the silicon and sixty per cent. of the phosphorus which existed in the pig iron were driven into the run-out cinder.

Through the courtesy of the Trenton Iron Company we have received valuable data concerning their working with scrap, hot and cold run-out metal.

In the following statements the quantities were furnished by the company, the prices we filled in. We presume a difference should have been made in the charge of sinking of perhaps $1 in favor of hot run-out.

In these works the metal is not allowed to get cold. The blooms are taken direct from the hammer, placed in a "wash" heating furnace, and the forgemen are paid per ton of 2,240 lbs. of billets. Therefore, no bad blooms are paid for.

Working Hot Run-out Metal.

1,282 tons pig, @ 1½c., ...	$19 23
960 lbs. coke, @ ¼c., ...	2 40
31 bush. charcoal, @ 6c., ...	1 86
Wages:	
Running-out, ...	1 50
Sinking, ...	5 50
Stocking R. O. and forge fires, ...	70
Hammering, wash-heating, and rolling, ...	3 95
Coal, .65 tons, (heat and power,) @ $5, ...	3 25
Repairs and general expenses, ...	4 50
Cost of 1 ton 1½ inch billets, ...	$42 89

Working Cold Run-out Metal.

1,282 tons pig, @ 1½c.,	$19 23
900 lbs. coke, @ ¼c.,	2 25
60 bush. charcoal, @ 6c.,	3 60
Wages:	
Running-out,	1 00
Sinking,	5 50
Stocking R. O. and forge fires,	80
Hammering, wash-heating and rolling,	3 95
Coal, .65 tons, (heat and power,) @ $5,	3 25
Repairs and general expenses,	4 50
Cost of 1 ton 1½ inch billets,	$44 08

Working No. 2 Scrap.

1,282 tons pig, @ 1½c.,	$19 23
34½ bush. charcoal, @ 6c.,	2 07
Wages:	
Stocking fires,	75
Sinking,	3 50
Hammering, wash-heating, and rolling,	3 95
Coal, .65 tons, (heat and power,) @ $5,	3 25
Repairs and general expenses,	4 50
Cost of 1 ton 1½ inch billets,	$37 25

In the Welsh forges the metal is run hot from the "run-out," or as it is there called, "dandy-fire," into the forge fires.

These thoughts have been given to present the matter to bloomary managers. We know of but the two places named where hot run-out is used in this country. One of these establishments maintains the fires, but does not use them at present. The other has them in use, and Mr. Smucker, the manager, claims material saving by them.

The cupola run-out, described on page 16 of No. 1 Journal, has given satisfaction by its operation at Potomac forge. In reference to its economy, Messrs. Agnew write: "One trial of it shows considerable saving in coal and iron, from any comparisons which we could make."

The practical economies can only be tested by extended experiment, and the data herein given will give ample opportunity for further investigation and discussion.

Words of Cheer.

So many encouraging notices from the *Press* met the first issue of our "Journal," that we can scarcely select from them without doing injustice. We return thanks for the favorable reception of the "Journal," and for the many personal compliments tendered. The kindly advice given by the *Mining Record* is so appropriate, that we desire all interested in the business to read it, and therefore, place it before them.

After referring to the "Journal" and the Association, the editor says:

"Certainly, this country of all that are included in that division of the globe known as 'Christendon,' is the one that most needs such an association. But we hope that the membership will include other persons than those who have a mere pecuniary interest in the subject of charcoal iron making, or else that these gentlemen of business will recognize the fact that their interests include things that are not to be measured by direct application of the dollar.

"In undertaking to organize the energies of this branch of manufacture, the association must remember that there are grave responsibilities connected with the task. The make of charcoal iron is limited, but the questions connected with its manufacture include the widest interest in metallurgy, both practical and scientific.

"Charcoal is the ideal blast furnace fuel. More iron can be made from a ton of it than from any other. In spite of its great bulk, more metal can be produced from a cubic foot of furnace room with this, than with any other fuel. Its product is the strongest known. It is the only fuel that does not add impurity to the metal made, and the only one that requires no flux on its own account. Finally, to this list of its perfections must be added its monopoly of the mysterious alchemistry of chilling, a phenomenon of which the world has taken advantage for a century, but really does not understand even at the present day.

"There is a reason for all this train of excellencies, and that reason is necessarily included in the peculiar conditions of charcoal as a form of carbon, and its adaptation to the artificial conditions of the blast furnace. Charcoal being a fuel of maximum perfection, it is evident that the law of combustion, as a practical, as distinguished from a scientific question, is to be discovered by the study of its prominence. Something has been done in this direction. Birkinbine, Church, and others have tried to point out the conditions and causes of its superiority, but much remains to be done. We trust that the new society will take measures to encourage investigation. It will pay. The vast economies which are every day reducing the cost of other irons, have not been applied to this, for fear of losing the valuable qualities which alone make the sale of charcoal pig possible at the high ruling prices. But, gentlemen of the association, that result is not inevitable. If we judge by what has been done in other departments of iron production, you can advance to a cheaper manufacture without losing any advantages of quality. At all events, in uniting under the sign of the *Charcoal Pig*, you have taken up this question, and now it behooves you to carry it on with spirit, to success."

The Oswego Furnace, in Oregon, which we described in our first issue, blew in May 29, with the furnace remodeled.

Mr. Creichton writes: "We put up a new engine with two cylinders, 5 feet stroke, 4 feet in diameter, with receiver 25×6 feet, run by a 30½-inch Leffell turbine water-wheel, in iron case, under a 40-foot head, giving us 147 horse power. Put in hearth of Scotch brick, new inwall, remodeled our hot blast, and put in a bell and hopper. Height of furnace now 44 feet; diameter of bosh, 10 feet; diameter of tunnel head, 6 feet. Blow through three 4-inch tuyeres. The second week produced 116¾ tons; largest yield of one day, 23¾ tons. We expect to turn out 140 to 150 tons of iron every week. Have a Blake ore crusher in bridge house to crush the raw ore as used; run by wire rope ½-inch in diameter; 150 feet from water wheel. Have 14,000 cords wood cut, and charcoal coming in fast. We have built a narrow-guage railroad, 2⅝ miles long, from furnace to ore mine, using T rail 30 pounds to yard. The cars run in ore shed on trestle work, 12 feet high, and dump in the bottom, letting the ore fall through. One man with one yoke of cattle hauls the iron to the river and takes out the cinder. We are making our calculations to keep the furnace running the year round; but our greatest drawback here is a lack of experienced men for coaling hands. Our colliers have to work too many green men."

Howard Furnace, Ohio, was put in blast July 5, and is doing well, making 15 tons mill iron per day. The furnace is 36 feet × 10 feet 8 inches.

Items of Interest about Charcoal Iron Works.

With the intention of keeping our members posted as to happenings at the various iron works, we shall in each issue give such facts as we become cognizant of in the interval.

We have information concerning damaging fires at three iron works. On June 8, the "Excelsior" furnace, at Ishpeming, Mich., operated under lease by the Carp River Iron Company, caught fire from sparks being thrown on a shingle roof by a slip in the furnace. The hoist, engine-house, and roof of casting house, (the walls are of stone,) were consumed, the stock-house was damaged, and the blowing machinery ruined. The loss will probably amount to $20,000, partially insured. Immediate preparations were made to re-build, and new machinery was procured. No coal was destroyed.

The Windsor (cold-blast) furnace, in Berks county, Pa., lost its water-wheel and wooden blowing-tubs, by sparks resting on wooden roofs setting fire to the buildings.

A load of charcoal lying outside the coal-house of the Big Pond furnace, Cumberland county, Pa., communicated fire to the buildings during the night of May 21. Owing to the dry weather, and the wind blowing at the time, the fire spread rapidly. The two coal-houses, bridge-house, and engine-house, were destroyed, and a neat steam engine and a pair of iron-blast cylinders ruined. In fact, nothing but the stone stack and boilers remain. Sixteen thousand bushels of coal, stocked, were on fire, but by promptly covering with clay, and drawing the following week as in pit burning, about 70 per cent. of the coal was saved.

The furnace had been thoroughly overhauled and put into good order by Messrs. C. V. Ahl & Son, who expected to blow in on June 1, had not the fire occurred.

It is doubtful if the furnace will be re-built, as Messrs. Ahl were only lessees, and have removed the ore and coal to their Carlisle iron works, at Boiling Springs.

The old Rolling-mill furnace at Marquette is about starting in with charcoal, having been leased by the Carp River Iron Company.

The Bloomery furnace, in Hampshire county, W. Va., has been re-built, and is now 9×40 feet. It will be operated by the Bloomery Furnace Company of Philadelphia, and make car-wheel iron.

One of L'Islet furnaces at Three Rivers, Canada, has been remodeled. It is now a cupola stack resting on iron columns, and is 8×40 feet. A new hot oven has also been built.

Major Pickands seems determined to wear the laurels for superior work in a charcoal furnace. We had scarcely come to appreciate his good work at Spring Lake furnace, when we received the following extracts from his annual report of the operation of Bangor furnace, Mich., size 43×110 feet:

Record of Bangor Furnace for 12 *months ending June* 30, 1880.

Tons of ore smelted,	24,596.3
Bushels of coal consumed, (2,748 cubic inches,)	1,458,350
Tons of limestone flux used,	841
Gross tons of pig iron made,	14,653½
Charges run,	58,334
Bushels of coal used per ton of iron made,	99.52
Average yield of ore, per cent.,	59.57
Pounds of flux per ton of iron,	134
Average burden carried, pounds,	946
Cubic feet of air used per ton of iron,	104,242
Pounds of air per pound of iron,	3.53

Number of days run, ...	352.3
Average daily product, gross tons, ...	41.54
Number of days run on this blast, ...	389.3
Tons of iron made on this blast, ...	15,950½

Furnace still in and averaging 43 tons daily. Best week's work, 356 gross tons.

There are a number of unusual points in this record: The amount of iron made, low fuel consumption, (about 2,000 lbs. charcoal per ton of iron,) small quantity of flux required, and the remarkable richness of the ores, are among these. But to us, the most surprising is the very small amount of air taken—about 52 cubic feet per pound of charcoal. This is less than any record we have ever seen. The blast is heated in iron pipe-stoves, and probably averages 850° F.

Mr. George D. Colby reports that he has been getting some extraordinary work out of the "Katahdin" furnace, in Maine, his record showing a product of from 14 to 18 tons of car-wheel iron per day, and 121 tons per week, with 83.3 bushels (2,680 cubic inches) of charcoal made from ⅓ poplar and ⅔ birch and maple. The ore yields from 52 to 61 per cent., averaging 54.42. Five hundred and fifty-five pounds limestone, and 52 pounds manganese are used per ton of iron. The average blast pressure is reported as 1.86 pounds, and the average temperature of blast 465° F. The furnace is 50 feet high and 10 feet diameter of bosh.

The "Hunnewell" furnace, Kentucky, is 45 feet high and 12½ feet bosh, open top; hot-blast, blown by two 4-inch tuyeres.

Mr. S. Eifurt, superintendent, furnishes us with figures showing the operation of the furnace. In 250 days 4,350 tons (2,268 lbs.) of pig iron were made—an average of 17.4 tons per day—using 3.1 tons of ore and 150 bushels of charcoal per ton of iron, the percentage of limestone used being 20.

An addition to the charcoal iron trade is a furnace at Clipper Gap, California, now being constructed.

Forest Fires.

Where timber is large and undergrowth light the danger from forest fires, and the loss accompanying them, is not as great as where the timber is younger and the brush heavier, but the fire risk is one common to all charcoal iron workers.

During this year the woodland fires have, in many localities, been unusually disastrous, and the association was able to render assistance to the charcoal iron trade of Pennsylvania and others, by discovering and printing the laws of the State which had been inoperative for want of receiving proper publicity. Copies of these laws were sent to every iron worker in Pennsylvania, and to all members of the association; and the press of the State gave proper prominence to them. The protection of our timbered areas from fire is of great importance, not only to our industry, but also to the community at large, and, appreciating this fact, we have collected, as far as possible, the laws of various States pertaining to forest fires, and give in the following pages a synopsis of the same. We shall be gratified to receive information from other States, or to have errors corrected in those published.

Maine leads off with a strong law which we give entire:

Revised Statutes, Chap. 26.

SEC. 19. If any person kindles a fire by the use of firearms in hunting or fishing, or any other means, on land not his own, without consent of the owner, he shall forfeit ten dollars; and if such fire spread or does any damage to the property of others, he shall forfeit a sum of not less than ten and not more than five hundred dollars, according to aggravation of the offense, and in either case shall stand committed until the fine and costs are paid.

SEC. 20. If any person, with intent to injure another, kindles or causes to be kindled a fire on his own or another's property, and thereby the property of any other person is injured or destroyed, he shall be punished by a fine of not less than twenty nor more than one thousand dollars, or by imprisonment of not less than three months nor more than three years, according to aggravation of the offense.

SEC. 21. Whoever, for a lawful purpose, kindles a fire on his own land shall do so at a suitable time and in a careful and prudent manner; and shall be liable, in action on the case to any person injured by his failure to comply with this provision.

SEC. 22. Persons engaged in driving lumber upon any waters may kindle fires when necessary for the purposes in which they are engaged, but shall use the utmost caution to keep them from spreading and doing damage, and if they fail to do so, they shall be subject to all the liabilities and penalties hereof, as if the privilege granted by this section had not been allowed.

SEC. 23. The common law right to an action for damages done by fires is not hereby taken away or diminished, but it may be pursued notwithstanding the penalties herein set forth, but any person availing himself of the provisions of section 21 shall be barred of his action by common law for the damage so sued for, and no action shall be brought at common law for kindling fires in the manner described in section 22; but if any such fire spreads and does damage, the person who kindled it, and any person present or concerned in driving the lumber, by whose act or might such fire is suffered to do damage, shall be liable in an action on the case for the damage thereby sustained.

The laws of Pennsylvania in reference to forest fires are, first: An act, approved March 31, 1860.

SEC. 140. If any person shall willfully set on fire, or cause to be set on fire, any woods, lands, or marshes within this Commonwealth, so as thereby to occasion loss, damages or injury to any other person, he or she shall be guilty of a misdemeanor, and on conviction, be sentenced to pay a fine not exceeding one hundred dollars, and to undergo an imprisonment not exceeding twelve months.—*Pamphlet Laws, 1860, page 416.*

This was followed in 1869 by a special act, applicable to Union county, which made the maximum fine five hundred dollars, and minimum imprisonment thirty days.

An act to protect timber lands from fire, approved June 2, 1870, is quite important, as it places the responsibility of at least assisting to control forest fires on the counties. It reads:

Whereas, It is important to the people of the State that timber lands should be protected from fire, which, owing to malicious conduct and carelessness of individuals, is causing vast havoc to the young growing timber, especially upon our mountains; therefore,

SEC. 1. *Be it enacted, &c.*, That *it shall be the duty of the commissioners of the several counties* of this Commonwealth to *appoint persons under oath*, whose duty it shall be to *ferret out and bring to punishment* all persons who either *willfully or otherwise* cause the burning of timber lands, and to *take measures to have such fires extinguished* where it can be done; the *expenses thereof to be paid out of the county treasury*, the unseated land tax to be the first applied to such expenses.

Section two extends the benefit of the special law for Union county to five others.

The latest law of this State on this subject was approved June 11, 1879, and is as follows:

SEC. 1. *Be it enacted, &c.*, That any person or persons who shall wantonly and willfully kindle any fire on the lands of another, so as to set on fire any wood lands, barrens or moors, within the limits of this Commonwealth, shall be guilty of a misdemeanor, and on conviction thereof shall be sentenced to pay a fine not exceeding *three hundred dollars*, and undergo an imprisonment not exceeding *twelve months*, or either, or both, at the discretion of the court; and prosecutions for such offenses may be commenced at any time within two years from the commission thereof.

SEC. 2. Upon the conviction of any person or persons for any of the offenses aforesaid, the commissioners of the county in which such conviction is had, shall *pay to the prosecutor* in every such case the sum of *fifty dollars* out of the county treasury as a reward for the apprehension and conviction of the offender, and the defendant or defendants shall pay the same, with the costs, as in other cases, into the hands of the sheriff for the use of the county, and nothing herein contained shall prevent the prosecutor from being a competent witness in the prosecution aforesaid.—*Pamphlet Laws, 1879, page 162.*

Virginia gives the miscreant who attempts such vandalism a fairly severe punishment, viz:

"If any person unlawfully and maliciously set fire to any woods, fence, grass, straw, or other thing capable of spreading fire on lands, he shall be fined not exceeding one hundred dollars, and shall be punished with stripes."—*Sessions, acts* 1874, *page* 64; 1877–8, *page* 287, § 7.

"If any person carelessly, negligently, or intentionally set any woods or marshes on fire, or set fire to any stubble, brush, straw, or inflammable substance capable of spreading fire on lands, whereby damage is done to the property of another, he shall, besides being liable in damages to the party so injured, be deemed guilty of a misdemeanor, and be fined not less than ten nor more than one hundred dollars."—*Sessions, acts* 1877–8, *page* 288, § 8.

The laws on this subject in Alabama are, 1st, a special act No. 124, approved March 28, 1873:

"SEC. 1. *Be it enacted by the General Assembly of Alabama,* That from and after the passage of this act it shall be unlawful for any person to burn or set fire to any wood within five miles of the coaling ground of any company making iron, or preparing to make the same, within the limits of the counties of Jefferson and Tuscaloosa, unless the consent of such company be obtained thereto.

"SEC. 2. *Be it further enacted,* That any person or persons violating the provisions of the foregoing section of this act, shall be guilty of a misdemeanor, and, upon conviction, shall be fined not exceeding five thousand dollars, and may be imprisoned in the county jail not exceeding ninety days, at the discretion of the court trying the same.

"SEC. 3. *Be it further enacted,* That for the conviction of each defendant under the provisions of this act, the solicitor shall be entitled to a fee of twenty dollars, to be taxed as costs against each defendant, and collected as in other cases of misdemeanors; *Provided,* That this act does not apply to teamsters.

A special act for Washington county, limited to three years, was passed in 1875 and repealed in 1877.

Revised Statutes of Alabama, Ed. 1876.

SEC. 4426. (Old Sec. 3743.) *Burning Woods.*—Any person who willfully sets fire to the woods or forests or uninclosed lands not belonging to himself, or willfully causes fire to be communicated to such woods or forests, (except during the months of February and March,) must, upon conviction, be fined not less than ten nor more than two hundred dollars.

Sec. 4427. (Old Sec. 3744.) *Burning of Pine Forests willfully.*—Any person who willfully sets fire to any pine forest which is used for the purpose of producing turpentine, with the intent to injure or destroy the same, must, upon conviction, be fined not less than one hundred, nor more than one thousand dollars, and may also be imprisoned in the county jail, or sentenced to hard labor for the county for not more than twelve months.

Sec. 4428. (Old Sec. 3745.) *Burning Pine Forest negligently.*—Any person who negligently or carelessly causes fire to be communicated to any pine forest which is used for the purpose of producing turpentine, and thereby destroy or injure the same, must, upon conviction, be fined not less than fifty dollars, nor more than five hundred dollars.

The law of Kentucky in reference to forest fires is found in General Statutes, Art. XXVIII, Chap. 29, page 358, and reads:

Sec. 5. If any person shall unlawfully set fire to any woods, fence, grass, straw, or other thing capable of spreading fire on land, he shall be fined not exceeding one hundred dollars.

Sec. 6. If any person intentionally or negligently set any woods on fire, whereby damage is done to the lands or property of another, he shall be fined at the discretion of a jury.

As far as we could learn, Ohio has only one enactment, which is as follows:

"Sec. 4. Whoever maliciously, or negligently, sets fire to any woods, prairies, or grounds, not his own property, or maliciously permits any fire to pass from his own prairies or grounds, to the injury or destruction of the property of any other person, shall be fined not more than one hundred dollars, or imprisoned not more than twenty days, or both."—*Ohio Laws, vol. 74, page 248.*

There were produced last year in Pennsylvania 27,825,000 gross tons of anthracite coal. This makes the total out-put of the anthracite coal region to date 427,987,832 gross tons. Of this the Schuylkill region has furnished 174,356,236 tons, the Wyoming region 172,944,369 tons, and the Lehigh region 80,687,227 tons.

Ancient Charcoal Iron.

The arrival of the Egyptian obelisk at New York revives the interest connected with the piece of iron reported to have been found under it.

This specimen was analyzed by Dr. A. Wendel, chemist of the Albany and Rennslaer Iron and Steel Company. In sending the JOURNAL a copy of his analysis, he remarks:

"From the physical appearance of the specimen, I am led to believe that the iron or steel had been in a molten state once, and therefore I had a right to assume it to be of meteoric origin. The analysis dispelled this view by not showing more cobalt and nickel.

"Certainly the steel must have been manufactured by a direct proces, *i. e.*, it was made from charcoal bloom by carburization. If so, this would be a very interesting contribution to ancient history."

The following is Dr. Wendel's analysis:

Iron,	98.738
Carbon,	0.521
Sulphur,	0.009
Silica,	0.017
Phosphorus,	0.048
Nickel, Cobalt,	0.079
Maganese,	0.116
Copper,	0.102
Calcium,	0.218
Magnesium,	0.028
Aluminum,	0.070
Slag,	0.150
	100.096

As an indication of the amount of timber cut for railway purposes, we find in the daily papers a statement that this year 500,000 railroad sills were shipped from Muskegon, Michigan, and this is only one of the numerous shipping points.

TUTTLE-NY

SUCH great advantages have been gained by the use of rock-drills in mining, that we believe our readers will be interested in the illustration of Clayton's Duplux Air Compressor, which is used to operate the drills. The inlet and discharge valves are small metal disks, and are shown in the exposed end of the air cylinder. The cylinders are provided with channeled water jackets to keep them cool. The piston rods of the two cylinders are connected by a double cross-head, to the steam end of which is attached a connecting rod operating the fly wheel through a crank.

These compressors are arranged to work under 60 to 100 lbs. air pressure, and are provided with steam and air governors.

They are built by the Clayton Steam Pump Works, in Brooklyn, New York.

Welding Iron and Steel.

In a discussion upon the welding properties of iron and steel, the *Iron Age* gives the opinions of a number of German engineers. So much of importance is connected with this property of wrought iron, and so great interest at present attaches to any comparison between the practical manipulations of iron and steel that we give place to some of the testimony of the German experts.

The welding of iron is dependent upon its property to assume a pasty state within a certain range of temperature, and it may be stated, in a general way, that the facility with which the welding may be performed is dependent upon the duration of this peculiar condition. Leaving out of consideration other circumstances affecting welding, it is conceded by the majority of metallurgists that an increase in the percentage of carbon in the iron impairs the property of welding, and it is generally believed that when two per cent. is reached it ceases entirely. It might be concluded that, therefore, it is desirable to keep the carbon within the lowest limits attainable, but there is some diversity of opinion on this point, because a second important condition for good welding comes into play. It is necessary, in order to unite two pieces of iron, to make the surfaces to be welded free from any coating of oxide, and some hold that a certain percentage of carbon is necessary in order to afford material for the reduction of this oxide. Wedding, among others, maintains that such is not the case, and that the silicate of iron contained in wrought iron plays an important rôle.

These theoretical considerations have quite recently become of considerable interest, because they may offer a clew to detecting the reason why the steel produced by the open-hearth and Bessemer processes is generally inferior as regards welding power to wrought iron, an inferiority which stands in the way of the more general adoption of steel in the place of wrought iron. The former, it is true, can be welded, but there are many practical difficulties. Certainly steel-headed rails show a case of good welding, and tires, tubes, &c., have been made of Bessemer steel on a large scale, but still steel connot compare in this respect with wrought iron. Herr Petersen claims that silicon is injurious, while Herr Koehler, of Bonn, held that it was not alone not injurious, but actually favorable for good welding. Herr Helmuth took a different view, and stated that at Bochum, during a series of experiments, in an open hearth furnace, they tried keeping the silicon low, but reached no results, and were similarly unsuccessful by increasing the percentage of phosphorus. They then turned to the Bessemer process and commenced overblowing, which improved the welding, though not in a sufficient degree. By using oxides of iron, however, they obtained much better results, but they did not follow out the matter, because they found that pieces welded together had a yellow red fracture near the weld, and Herr Gresser, of Grafenberg, added that the same tendency to red-shortness was observed by them when making a weldable material in the open-hearth furnace. In using the Terrenoire alloy they found that a good product was obtained by adding about four times as much manganese as silicon. It was, however, abandoned on account of its high price. Herr Petersen concludes by giving some interesting data in regard to the influence of arsenic upon the welding of iron. A lot of inch rod was rejected on account of difficulty in welding, and it was found that the heated rods had a fatty luster, and that two rods laid one upon another slid off as though the surface were polished. This took place, although the balls in the puddling furnace and the piles welded well. The cause of this anomaly was found to be that the injurious effect of the arsenic comes out strongly only after the carbon has been considerably reduced. The following analyses are given as representing the composition of the pig used in making these rods, the first being white, the second gray pig:

Sulphur,	0.774	1.843
Phosphorus,	trace	trace
Copper,	0.090	0.580
Arsenic,	4.250	5.980
Antimony,	1.145	1.068

Correspondence.

One of our members makes the following suggestion, which we commend to our readers as an indication of how they can each advance the interest of the JOURNAL:

"How would it do to have part of a column headed '*Quere*,' and under this head ask pertinent questions interesting to the association withont answer. It might induce replies from numbers who will otherwise be mum. For instance, for the transportation of charcoal long distances, is a two, four, or six horse team most economical?

"Were springs ever used on charcoal wagons of over 200 bushels capacity?

"Is there any advantage in having the rear bolster of a charcoal wagon higher than front bolster?

"Is there a better mode of unloading coal wagons than with bottom draw boards, in order to save the crushing of coal with the wagon wheels?

"What size, kind, and shape of house is best to stock charcoal in?

"In a blast furnace, is not a forehearth, tymp, and dam each superfluous?

"Of what use were or are the buck walls, common to old fashioned charcoal furnaces?

"Is a casing of any kind, outside and around the lining, boshes, or hearth of a blast furnace necessary, or is it possibly a positive injury?

" What material is the best for the bottom of a runout fire?

" Is a double forge or finery fire superior to a single fire? And so on."

Quotations.

August 14, 1880.

From data received, we are able to report a decided stiffening in the market, and comparatively light stocks. The largest accumulation of which we have knowledge, being in Northwestern Ohio.

We have quotations of New England car wheel irons, warm blast, $40 to $42; New York ore blooms for steel are selling at $57 50 to $60; cold blast Pennsylvania car wheel iron is quoted at $38 to $40 at furnace; charcoal plate slabs and bloom, $70 per 2,464 lbs., and run out anthracite blooms, $56.

Baltimore and Lake Superior hot blast car wheel irons are bringing $42 cash.

Alabama hot blast foundry is selling at from $23 to $28; car wheel iron, $40.

Ohio Hanging Rock car wheel cold blast, $47 at Cincinnati.

Kentucky Hanging Rock foundry is quoted @ $28 and $30, 4 months.

Most of our correspondents report improved demand.

Notes.

The census bureau has prepared a preliminary catalogue of the forest trees of North America, embracing 342 varieties.

Of the Cupuliferæ, of which the oak and beech are members, there are forty varieties, thirty-four of which are oaks. There are eleven varieties of the Betulaceæ, or birch and alders; sixty-four varieties of Coniferæ are noticed, of which twenty-eight are pines and the balance are varieties of the larch, spruce, hemlock, cypress, cedar, and juniper trees; ten varieties of ash; five of elm; four of walnut; seven of hickory; seven of maple—are among those described.

From this preliminary publication, which has been extensively distributed, it is the intention to complete a correct list of all forest trees in the United States, giving their extreme geographical range, and points of greatest perfection, dimensions of remarkable species, common or local names in connection with botanical names; uses to which the wood has been put, and products obtained from it. Such a report will be of material value to all owners of forest lands, and our efforts will be devoted to giving our members the advantage of all such information accessible.

DR. ANGUS SMITH claims to have made the interesting discovery that charcoal absorbs gases in definite volumes, the physical action resembling the chemical. Calling the volume of hydrogen absorbed 1, the volume of oxygen absorbed is 8; that is, while hydrogen unites with eight times its weight of oxygen to constitute water, charcoal absorbs eight times more oxygen by volume than it absorbs hydrogen. The specific gravity of oxygen being sixteen times greater than hydrogen, charcoal absorbs eight times sixteen, or one hundred and twenty-eight times more oxygen, by weight, than it does hydrogen, and so on.

AN EXPLOSION OF A BLAST FURNACE, of uncommon character, took place recently, at Marnaval Saint-Dizier, France. The furnace being in blast as usual, a sudden explosion carried away the top of the furnace, and split it down to within thirty feet of the hearth. For a short time it behaved like a very volcano, vomiting stones, ore, molten pig, and white-hot coke, and scattering its contents some five hundred yards around. Ten persons were hurt. The accident is supposed to have had its origin in the boshes getting choked, so that an explosive mixture was formed within the furnace.

HUGO SÖDERSTRÖM claims that good and much cheaper dyes than are produced from some of the exotic plants generally employed, can be made from the wood of mulberry and acacia trees, dried pear leaves, oak bark, bark and young shoots of poplar, juniper berries, sorrel roots and several of the common weeds.—*Frank. Inst. Jour.*

THE following table is an extract from a paper read before the "American Association for Advancement of Science," by Prof. R. H. Thurston, of Hoboken, New Jersey:

KIND OF TIMBER.	TENSILE TESTS.				COMPRESSION TESTS.			TRANSVERSE STRESS.	
	Diameter in decimal of an inch.	Tensile strength in pounds.	Total elongation in inches and decimals.	Weight per cubic foot in pounds.	Diameter in inches and decimals.	Compressive strength in pounds.	Compression per cent. of length.	Load.	Deflection.
White Pine, .	0.527	6,877.5	0.725	29.376	1.117	9,592.6	3.498	5,280	1.28
Yellow Pine,	0.532	2,070.2	1.650	46.656	1.102	11,952.3	2.906	16,740	1.96
Locust, .	0.522	28,925.2	1.850	57.024	1.073	14,818.9	3.300	13,680	2.70
Black Walnut,	0.535	9,786.4	0.850	38.016	1.112	7,001.7	1.254	7,440	0.72
White Ash, .	0.544	15,940.5	1.475	34.560	1.104	8,148.3	2.310	9,720	2.50
White Oak, .	0.481	13,207.8	1.300	41.472	1.117	7,143.5	3.300	9,840	1.76
Live Oak, . .	0.497	10,309.2	1.150	67.392	1.117	10,409.2	3.366	11,280	1.38

The length of pieces subjected to tensile test was 4 inches.

The length of pieces subjected to compression test was 2¼ inches.

The size of pieces subjected to transverse test was 54 inches long by 3 inches square.

A REPORT has been issued, giving the results of the inquiries conducted at the Royal Victoria Hospital, Netley, as to the relative efficacy of materials used in filters. The object was to ascertain what were most suited for used by the Admiralty and the War Office. Animal charcoal, carferal, (a mixture of carbon, iron, and alumina,) silicated carbon, and spongy iron were tested in several series of experiments, and the data obtained are given in many columns of figures. Out of the fifteen series of experiments, carferal came out first in thirteen, and silicated carbon in two. The adoption of carferal was recommended, though the exact proportions of the mixture were not decided upon.—*Iron Age.*

ERRATA.

Page 6, paragraph 2, for " 3.16 " read " 31.6."

Page 7, paragraph 1, for " 1870 " read " 1879."

Page 11, last paragraph, for " 48 diameter " read " 48 inches diameter."

The matter on pages 33 and 34, referring to Oswego and Howard furnaces, should appear under head of " Items of Interest about Charcoal Iron Works."

Page 35, paragraph 6, for " 110 feet " read " 10 feet."

JOURNAL

OF

UNITED STATES ASSOCIATION

OF

CHARCOAL IRON WORKERS.

EDITED BY THE SECRETARY.

No. 3. NOVEMBER, 1880.

MOST of the space in this number is devoted to the minutes of the annual meeting, a narrative of the proceedings, the President's annual address, and some of the papers which were read at the meeting, giving a volume considerably larger than has been our custom.

We regret that it was impossible to incorporate all of the papers, and the discussions upon them, but the balance will appear in No. 4, about the first of the new year, and will be found fully as interesting as those here given. Future numbers will contain monographs upon subjects suggested by the papers and discussions.

We shall be pleased to have the readers of the JOURNAL send us data, either verifying or controverting the experiences or investigations given by the writers of the various papers. Our object is mutual improvement, and for all to share in these benefits. All who have facts or data should contribute them to the general fund.

Minutes of the Annual Meeting.

FIRST SESSION.

Pursuant to call of the executive committee, the Charcoal Iron Workers of the United States met in annual session at Harrisburg, Pennsylvania, Tuesday evening, October 19, 1880, and, at eight o'clock, P. M., were called to order in the Young Men's Christian Association hall, Colonel George P. Wiestling presiding.

The Association was welcomed to Harrisburg by His Honor Mayor John D. Patterson, in the following words:

MR. PRESIDENT AND MEMBERS OF THE UNITED STATES ASSOCIATION OF CHARCOAL IRON MANUFACTURERS, LADIES AND GENTLEMEN: It has often been my pleasant duty to extend, on behalf of the people of this city, a welcome to the representatives of various societies assembled here for the deliberation of questions and matters pertaining to their order; but on this occasion, and to this particular body of representative gentlemen, we may be pardoned for being somewhat selfish, as we esteem it not only an honor and pleasure to extend a cordial welcome, but that it is to our interests as a people and a municipality to have assembled in our midst a body of men representing an industry with a record of its productions dating back to 1810, and an organization representing a business extending over twenty-two States, and one that requires the expenditure of millions of dollars of capital annually, and the services of men of energy and of executive ability to successfully conduct it. For these and other reasons, I am here in the name of the people of Harrisburg to tender to you a cordial and hearty greeting of welcome to their hospitalities. May your visit here be enjoyable to you, and your sessions beneficial to the industries you represent. We also trust that while you are here temporarily you may be enabled to ascertain, and be favorably impressed, with the many advantages which this city, and its location, offers you to become permanent residents thereof, and active factors in the thriving industries of the same. To you all, welcome. [Applause.]

To the address of welcome, the President responded as follows:

In the behalf of the United States Association of Charcoal Iron Workers, I beg to assure your Honor, the mayor of this, the capital city of the great Keystone State, that we are deeply sensible of the honor you have done us by your presence at our meeting; that we fully appreciate the kindly words you have spoken, and sincerely thank you for the cordial welcome you have extended to us. And yet I may be pardoned for adding that being somewhat acquainted with your official and personal reputation, knowing of the hospitality and generosity of the citizens of Harrisburg, among whom I passed the days of my boyhood, and familiar with the magnitude and success of your manufactures, and the pride and interest they afford your State, we anticipated that at least you would not be entirely indifferent to the objects which brought us here.

We are aware that vigor is not always with youth, neither does wisdom invariably attach to old age, still our young organization of but one year's existence represents that branch of iron manufactures whose history antedates all others. Our members represent almost every State in the Union, and there are among our number those who have been engaged in manufacturing charcoal iron for a longer period than the years of my whole pilgrimage.

My associates own, control, and manage large estates; they superintend great agricultural interests; they delve deep into the bowels of the earth, and wrest from Nature the hidden ores of iron; the music of their industries is heard in mines, quarries, and workshops; they furnish employment to a large number of men and horses; they harness both steam and the elements to do their bidding; they establish and support churches and schools; they manage furnaces, forges, and mills, and develop continually the wealth of the nation.

Nor are they void of sentiment amid all these practical surroundings, for their work carries them high up upon the mountain top, where the dignified pine stretches out its lofty branches to the sky; where, in the words of one of silvery tongue, "the Almighty distils that life-giving beverage, pure cold water; where the red deer wanders, and the child loves to play;" and where the streamlets, like "ribbons of silver," unwind and carry health and gladness and wealth to the fertile plains below. Familiar with grand and beautiful scenes in Nature, my associates have learned to love the beautiful, and admire the generous, and thus they are fitted to fully value the manifestations of your goodness given them to-night.

Permit me again to assure your Honor, Mayor Patterson; the committee of reception, who have done their work so kindly, so nobly, and so well; and the ladies and gentlemen who grace this hall, and honor us by their presence to-night, that we thank you sincerely now, and, after the objects of our gathering are accomplished, and we hie us away to our labors by the mountain, the lake, and the stream, that our memories will keep in view that the grandest lesson we learned at our annual meeting was that of generosity and hospitality, taught us by your noble hearts. [Applause.]

Colonel George B. Wiestling then read an interesting and valuable address to the Association, (which appears in this number of the JOURNAL.)

The reading of the minutes of the last meeting was, on motion, dispensed with, as they have been published in the JOURNAL.

On motion of Mr. Archibald McAllister, of Blair county, Pennsylvania, the Chair appointed a committee (Messrs. Archibald McAllister, Pennsylvania; J. P. Agnew, Virginia; and R. N. Gere, New York) to make nominations for the coming year.

The paper read was discussed by Messrs. Hildrup, Milnes, Coffin, Birkinbine, and Wiestling.

The committee on nominations reported for

President—Colonel George B. Wiestling, Pennsylvania.

Vice President—Honorable Willard Warner, Alabama.

Managers—Messrs. Owen W. Davis, Maine; Charles Blair, Connecticut; Cyrus Butler, New York; J. C. Fuller, Pennsylvania; Henry T. Townsend, Pennsylvania; A. G. Curtin, Jr., Pennsylvania; Robert Valentine, Pennsylvania; George C. Lobdell, Delaware; C. E. Coffin, Maryland; Hon. William Milnes, Jr., Virginia; Alfred L. Tyler, Alabama; Charles Campbell, Ohio; E. Peckham, Missouri; Hon. C. J. L. Meyer, Wisconsin;

H. A. Burt, Michigan; H. S. Pickands, Michigan; Seymour Brownell, Minnesota; E. W. Crichton, Oregon.

On motion of Mr. D. S. Hunter, of Pennsylvania, the nominations of the committee were made the unanimous choice of the Association, by acclamation.

Mr. John Birkinbine read a paper on the subject of "Our Fuel," (which will be published in a future issue of the Journal.)

The paper was discussed by Messrs. Charles Blair, Connecticut; George B. Wiestling, Pennsylvania; Owen W. Davis, Maine; and replies made by Mr. Birkinbine.

After announcing programme for the following day, the Secretary made allusion to the iron ores and the limestones of the vicinity and the fuel facilities of Harrisburg.

Adjourned.

SECOND SESSION.

The Association re-assembled for business in the court-house at Chambersburg, Pa., at 7.45 P. M., October 20.

After calling the body to order, President Wiestling said:

"I take great pleasure in introducing to the members of the Association, and the ladies and gentlemen present, a representative man of this county of Franklin, Pennsylvania—one who reflects the generous sentiment of this whole community—the president judge of this judicial district, the Honorable D. Watson Rowe."

When the applause given on his appearance had subsided, Judge Rowe said:

MR. PRESIDENT AND GENTLEMEN OF THE ASSOCIATION: I see by your programme that it was not thought necessary you should be welcomed in an address to Chambersburg and Franklin county; but our committee of reception, at a late moment, seemed to think it was altogether becoming and appropriate that some one, on behalf of this community, should welcome you to our town and to our valley, and they did me the honor to select me to be their spokesman in that regard; and I have now the pleasure—a decidedly very great pleasure—of welcoming you all to the town of Chambersburg, to the county of Franklin, and to the Cumberland Valley.

I notice by your programme that you call yourselves "The United States Association of Charcoal Iron Workers," and I am informed that many of you come from distant parts of the country—some for Minnesota, some from the New England States, and some from the Southern States—and that you have expressed and exhibited a great interest in the meetings which you have thus far held.

I suppose an association of this kind would not have been seen a dozen years ago. This illustrates one of the marked tendencies of the times—the tendency to union or aggregation. I think it may be seen in every department of life. In politics we notice that the smaller states are being absorbed and great nations formed. Witness Germany, witness Italy. In religion, after the Reformation, there was a tendency to pull apart, and towards individualism; but now the movement is the reverse, and we observe in great religious bodies a tendency to come together, and we have Pan-Anglican councils, and Pan-Presbyterian councils, and the like. I notice that there is a tendency towards the coming together of men in classes representing their social and industrial interests. The trade unions of England and America are evidence of this; and so it is, perhaps, in accordance with the tendency of things, or the spirit of the age, that you are drawn together; for very often those things which seem to be just the offspring of the individual will, or of the present moment, are the results of great forces, and sometimes even of cosmical forces.

I notice, also, that you call yourselves "workers." Perhaps I should not put too much stress upon the word "workers,"—"charcoal iron workers." Perhaps you had not much in view when you used that. Still, I am feign to believe that you intended all useful work as being honorable. Who is a worker? Not he only who works with his hands, but the mental worker—he who uses any faculty that God has given him, to ameliorate the condition of the human race. The man who makes two spears of grass grow where one grew before is a public benefactor; and a true worker is a well-doer. As I understand, you not only work with your brains, but with your brains you make others work; and they are your "hands:" You call them such, and rightly, because any one who does for another is the hand of another, though he be also working for himself. And this is the best style of work; for such a person not only provides work for his own hands, but puts others to work.

Now, then, you are iron men. You are identified with the great iron interests of the country. I need not enlarge upon that. Still, it is a great satisfaction to you, no doubt, to be conscious of the fact that you are engaged in so useful and honorable an occupation; not only one involving great sums, but of the highest usefulness to the community. I assert nothing extravagant when I say that iron manufacture is as important to the State as agriculture itself—for what would be the result if iron and its uses were obliterated. This is the age of iron, and that means this is the age of civilization. There was once a "golden age," sung by the poets. I know not whether it existed in the past. I put it in the future, as in dreamland, Then there was the "stone age"—one of barbarism; and then the "iron age." Civilization came in with the use of iron implements. Civilization depends on iron implements. Civilization will go out with iron. Therefore it is your avocation in life is highly useful, and, consequently, highly honorable.

I am glad that this is an association of workers in iron that I have to welcome to-night. I welcome you to a very beautiful valley—at least I have heard other strangers say as much, and I hope your own observations will bear them out, and that such impressions will be yours, when you leave us on your tour of visitation, inspection, and business. We have mountains, and woods, and waters, and quite a diversified scenery. That, perhaps, is not creditable to us; we did not make it—God did that. I think it is a matter of congratulation to *us* that we live in the midst of such beautiful surroundings.

I am glad to be able to welcome you to so beautiful a country. After all there is something in the surroundings within which we are living. The environment of a man molds his character. You know very well that the dwellers by the sea partake of the restlessness of the ocean, as notice the dwellers upon almost any coast. The inhabitants of the plain partake of the quiet of the plain itself. You know that the dwellers on the mountains are as free as the air they breathe; as independent as the eagles which soar around their mountain crags, and as hardy and sturdy in character as the mountains themselves. So there is something in the surroundings of men.

In this valley we have large iron deposits. That will be interesting to you. I know not how extensive they are, nor how rich. I shall not begin to talk iron in this presence any more than I would talk horse before a jockey club; but I will say, that eminent geologists tell us that much of our soil is underlaid with iron. In speaking of the formations at Mount Pleasant, they say that the deposits vary in depth from eighty feet upward, and that the ore beds of Mont Alto are a hundred feet thick. Some persons, who deem themselves authorized to speak, suppose that the day is not far distant when this valley will be dotted all over with furnaces, because we have everything here required for the economical production of iron, save coal. We have wood on our mountain sides and in our valleys still in large quantities, but we have no coal. We are down on the lower silurian. The coal measures were far above us, and they do not appear until we reach Broad Top or the Cumberland coal fields, not much further away, where there are vast deposits of coal. Some time this coal will be brought here, and then it is likely the smoke of many furnaces will ascend even from this valley.

You will visit, I understand, some of our iron works whilst you are here. Permit me to tell you in a general way what we have in that line, without giving particulars. You will fill up the details. Our oldest furnace in point of time is Richmond, now so called, but originally called Mount Pleasant. This furnace was erected by Williams, Benjamin, and George Chambers in the year 1783. They transmuted their ores there, and were very successful. That furnace has been in operation most of the time ever since. It is now owned by the Southern Pennsylvania Iron and Railroad Company, and very extensive improvements have been made there. A few miles above, in Path valley, a very beautiful valley, with a population as orderly, as intelligent, and as moral as can be found anywhere under the sun, is Carrick furnace, which was founded by General Samuel Dunn in 1828. Then coming to this side of the mountain, in St. Thomas township, you will find the Franklin furnace, founded by P. & G. Housum in 1828, now operated by Messrs. Hunter & Springer, of the committee who are receiving you now. As to the character of the products of this furnace, I need not speak to iron men.

Then coming to Chambersburg, you will find here the Falling Spring furnace. This is Messrs. Hunter & Springer's baby, lately christened. I happened to be present at the christening. They were at a loss for a name, but near by there is a stream of bright clear water that falls into the Conococheague, and they named it the "Falling Spring." Then you go on to Mont Alto, called "Hughes' furnace" for half a century. It was founded by Daniel and Samuel Hughes in 1808. Holker Hughes was for many years manager there. I remember him well, and I take pleasure in mentioning his name to you. The property now belongs to the Mont Alto Iron Company. It is under the management of Colonel Wiestling, who presides over you this evening. He has built a railroad, besides enlarging the works, and has laid out, and made popular, Mont Alto park, for want of something better to do in dull times. But I will say nothing further about Colonel Wiestling nor his park, for you will see them both, and they will speak for themselves. [Applause.] There is one thing about Mont Alto park that has always attracted my attention. I have never stood there, in those beautiful grounds, and gazed at the old South Mountain, but that I have felt I should take off my hat to that venerable object. Old South Mountain! It belongs to the laurentian system, the oldest rocks known to geology; and at a very early period in the history of the world it stood out there, towering up into the air as high as the Alps or the Andes do to-day. If you will let your imaginations for a moment paint the wonderful things that old mountain saw in the history of the world, and the history of man, you will also feel that it is a very venerable pile.

Leaving Mont Alto, and going a few miles to the south, you reach old Caledonia furnace, which is indissolubly connected with a name famous in American history, and one, I am glad to mention to-night, as linked with the iron-workers of America, the name of Thaddeus Stevens. [Great applause.] He was not a citizen of our county, nor born here, but he spent much of his life within our borders. He held a firm grasp on "old Caledonia," and never let it go in his life time. He seemed to be one of us, and we claim all that there was of him that made him an iron-worker. He lived in an important period of our nation's history. He had a great opportunity, as a leader in the lower House of Congress in the midst of the civil war, and he was equal to it. He was great enough for the occasion, and no man, I venture to say, ever wielded so powerful an influence in that branch of Congress as did he. He was called the "Old Commoner." [Applause.] He was the noblest Roman of them all. He had an iron will, a keen intellect. In addition to bright wit, he could use the deadliest sarcasm. He had the firmest grasp, but with all he had great power of organization and management —a faculty which, it seems to me, is largely developed by the occupation of the iron-worker. But I shall not say anything more about our iron furnaces, or the men connected with them.

And now, gentlemen, with the hope that some of you will come among us, and help to enliven our community in the early future, I welcome you to Chambersburg and to Franklin county, in the name of the people of this town and county, and I do it with all my heart. [Applause.]

A response on behalf of the Association to the generous welcome extended, was made by the Vice President, Honorable Willard Warner, of Alabama, as follows:

JUDGE ROWE AND CITIZENS OF CHAMBERSBURG AND FRANKLIN COUNTY: I was requested, at a very late hour this evening, to acknowledge, in behalf of this Association, the kindly welcome which has been given us. When I heard the very interesting, and instructive, and very eloquent speech of our friend Judge Rowe, in behalf of the people of Chambersburg and Franklin county, and knew that I had to respond, I felt very much like a friend of mine did in Philadelphia last February, at a meeting of an important commission, when he was called upon to make a speech without preparation, and unaccustomed to speaking. He said he could tell a story, where a friend was called upon to make a speech ; but he had a much longer notice than I had. He had time to prepare himself, and commit his speech to memory. So when the time arrived, he began with precision and strong assurance: "Ladies and Gentlemen: When this beautiful country around about us here, with all its wealth and luxury, and with its beautiful homes, was a howling wilderness"—there the speech left him; he had forgotten all the rest. After thinking a moment, he began again: "Ladies and Gentlemen: When this beautiful country around about us here, with all its wealth and luxury, and with its beautiful homes, was a howling wilderness"—and his speech left him again. The third time he started: "Ladies and Gentlemen: When this beautiful country around about us here, with all its wealth and luxury, and with its beautiful homes, was a howling wilderness—and darned if I don't wish it had stayed so!" [Laughter.] And I feel a little so when I am called upon to reply to the very beautiful speech which we have just heard.

But I feel I will have done a favored duty when I shall say in behalf of this Association, and every member of it, too, that we return our very sincere and heartfelt thanks to Judge Rowe, and to the people of Chambersburg and Franklin county, for their very kind and very hospitable welcome. I know I can say for myself, that it has been a very agreeable surprise to me, and I doubt not to every member of the Association, that the people of Chambersburg should have been so thoughtful and kind as to delegate one of their most distinguished citizens—a man in whom any who have never seen him before, recognize as one of the first men of the country—to come and formally welcome us here. I did not expect it. It was a pleasant surprise to us, and I can say, in behalf of all the members of the Association, that we return our very sincere thanks for this thoughtful kindness.

The judge has spoken about the great interest with which we are connected, and it is a great interest. It is an interest as closely connected with the welfare, the progress, the civilization, and the enlightenment of the human race, as any other industry on the earth. It has been well said that the course of the industry of iron has marked the civilization for ages and ages past. The forwardness of the iron industry has always been an indication of the condition of civilization and the enlightenment of the day, and it is a fair index of it to-day, ladies and gentlemen.

The fact that the iron interest of to-day stands far forward in its progress, in its possibilities, and in its results, is, of itself, an indication of the great strides, yea, the mighty strides, that the people of this country, and of the world, have made in all the arts and industries, and in all else that elevates, ennobles, and advances mankind.

But the work is not yet done. There is much yet to be learned; there is much progress yet to be made in iron making. For myself, being a comparative novice, I feel as though I were learning my A, B, C's. I know we have older heads present, who have spent a life-time in this industrial pursuit, and yet feel that they are groping their way along the the difficult path of iron making.

I may say, Judge Rowe, that the object of this Association is to bring together one branch of this great industry for intercommunication of thought on processes, and labors, and results, and thereby benefit each other, and thus be a benefit to our fellow men and our common country. I believe that underlying the business interests which, in some degree, move this Association, there is a better and a nobler purpose, and that is, to do every industry, and the whole country, a real good. [Applause.] Our meetings, our suggestions, our periodicals, are not alone for ourselves, but they are for the good and for the instruction of the whole country, and for everybody to see. We are beginning to appreciate our position; and we are organizing, as you have well said, realizing that every great work is carried on by organization and concentrated effort. We come together as an organization to forward our industry and to advance its interests. I came from Alabama, from that sunny clime, to hear and see what I can learn. I come to the great State of Pennsylvania, an empire in itself, which makes half the iron of a great country, whose annual production is over four million tons; a great country, which now has as many miles of railroad, within four thousand, as all Europe combined; a great country, which, in a few years, will outstrip the world in the magnitude of her iron industries and productions, and in the extent of her railroads. I come to this great State to see what your people, who are the fathers of this great industry, are doing, and to carry the information back to our sunny land for our profit and advancement. Our friend Mr. Milnes, one of the South's oldest citizens, comes here from Virginia to gain additional knowledge. Another friend, (Mr. Meyer,) has come here from far-distant Wisconsin, to see what we have learned, and to give what they have learned for our common benefit. It is really a noble work, if we are actuated by right purposes. If we appreciate the magnitude and the dignity of the objects of this Association, it is a grand work, and one in which we may well be proud; and I feel that our generous fellow-citizens here, of the people of Chambersburg and Franklin county, from appreciating this noble purpose we have in view, have gone to the pains of giving us this formal welcome here to-night. I hope we may be incited to greater effort and higher purposes by the fact that our work is appreciated in all that we may do in our Association for the benefit of every walk in life.

It is wonderful, when you look at this iron industry, to see how wisely has been distributed the several materials for the making of iron, not only in this country, but everywhere in the entire world—for everywhere you find them. With every day's demand for an increased production, there is opened up some where in the land facilities for an increased supply. With every day there are new methods and new processes of manufacture; and every day we move on in the march of progress; and the time is not far distant when this industry will spread over the entire world, even to distant regions where now it is unknown.

But I think Americans may say with truth, and without unreasonable boasting, that here in this favored land of ours, in this great free republic of ours, under that glorious star-spangled banner of ours, [applause,] we are destined to become the first iron producing country of this world, as we are now the first and the freest nation on the globe. [Renewed applause.]

Let me add a single word: My friend has alluded in eloquent terms to the "great commoner," Thaddeus Stevens. I remember him well, and I am very glad to be able to contribute a word to the extraordinary ability, the indomitable will, the mighty grasp of intellect, and the unflinching devotion to his country, which characterized him. I remember, too, the grim humor of the old man. I remember that once when he was being carried into the capitol by two stalwart men, he asked them: "Boys, what will you do when I'm gone?" He was not only a great man, but friendly to every great industry.

My friend well said that he "who causes two spears of grass to grow where but one grew before is a public benefactor," and that in that sense manufacturers of iron are public benefactors. They take from the earth that which lying there is useless and worthless, and, by their labor, their skill, and their intellect, make it valuable, useful, and beneficial to man. When benefactors of our race, we can more and more see and appreciate the dignity of our calling, and live more and more in accordance with its high purposes. Where so fitting a place that we should meet? Where so fitting a place that this Association should have had its origin, or its birth or inception, as in this great iron State of Pennsylvania? Here it was suggested, here it was born, and here it has grown into being. It is now living in its second year, but it has already become strong and stalwart, with every prospect of a still larger and more vigorous growth.

As it now exists before you, on behalf of the President and members of the Association, I tender to the people of the town of Chambersburg, of Franklin county, and of this broad, rich, and fertile valley, our very heart-felt thanks. [Applause.]

The President: "Ever since our first parents, Adam and Eve, committed that first sin in the garden, and the fiat went forth that man should live by the sweat of his face, weeds have grown spontaneously, and everything good has been contaminated with evil. So we find it in iron. One of the baneful impurities we meet with is sulphur, and the attention of the Association will be given to a paper on 'The Desulphurization of Iron Ores,' by Mr. O. W. Davis, of Bangor, Maine."

Mr. Davis then read his paper on "The Desulphurization of Ores," (which appears in this JOURNAL.)

Remarks were made thereon by Messrs. Wister, Davis, Meily, and Warner.

Mr. Le Compte C. Lewenhaupt (Swedish Minister to the United States) was called upon, and extended to the Association the good will of his country, which makes charcoal iron only.

The Association then discussed the subject of "The best Material or Composition for the Hearth of a Blast Furnace, where Charcoal is used," whether sandstone or fire-brick.

Remarks were made thereon by Messrs. Warner, Lobdell. Wiestling, McDougall, (Canada,) Coffin, Moore, and the Secretary.

The President announced that there was a gentleman present (Mr. J. A. Mathieu) who had an improved process for making charcoal in retorts, by which he claimed to have obtained a yield of 70 bushels to the cord, besides great economy in utilizing what otherwise would be refuse.

Mr. Birkinbine addressed he Association on the subject, by request of Mr. Mathieu, after which the Association adjourned.

After adjournment, Mr. Mathieu distributed circulars, and answered questions relative to his improved process of charcoal manufacture. (This apparatus will be treated of in a separate article in the future.)

THIRD SESSION.

The Association re-assembled for business at 8 o'clock, P. M., in the Young Men's Christian Association hall, Harrisburg.

The Secretary announced the reception of letters of regret from members of the Association who were not able to attend the sessions this year; also, the receipt of a number of circulars on peat charcoal and ore crushers, which were distributed to members.

Professor F. B. Hough, United States Commissioner of Forestry, was then introduced, and addressed the Association on the "Importance of giving timely Attention to the Growth of Woodlands for the Manufacture of Charcoal for Metalurgical Purposes."

The Professor, at the conclusion of his address, was heartily applauded.

The President said: Professor Hough, I do not know that I can, in any better way, express the thanks of this body for your able address than by saying that, in recognition of the importance of the subject which has been committed to your charge, and the ability which you bring to bear in your official duty, that this Association at its meeting last Tuesday night unanimously elected you an honorary and corresponding member thereof.

Professor Hough: I return my sincere thanks for this honor, which I consider the highest one that could be conferred.

The Association listened to the reading of a paper by the Secretary from Mr. Samuel Noble, of Alabama, entitled "Some Notes on the Styrian Forests."

Discussion ensued on both papers, participated in by Messrs. Meyer, Hough, Wiestling, Warner, Davis, Lobdell, Birkinbine, and Martin.

Mr. Willard Warner, of Alabama, offered the following resolution; which was unanimously adopted:

Resolved, That this Association earnestly favors the work of the Department of Agriculture in the matter of the preservation of American forests, and that we especially commend the steps taken by the Department to secure legislation to protect our forests from fire.

The Secretary made the following report of receipts and expenditures to October 1, 1880:

Receipts,		$477 00
Disbursements:		
Stationery,	$10 85	
Postage,	96 91	
Express,	2 75	
Printing,	227 56	
Engraving,	16 75	
Clerical labor,	12 60	
Expenses of meetings,	78 50	
Incidentals,	4 55	
		450 47
Balance on hand,		$26 53

A congratulatory telegram was received from Mr. Fuller, at Pine Grove, to which the Secretary was instructed to make reply.

Mr. John Milnes, of Virginia, called attention to the great diversity of weights in the special products of charcoal iron works, and questioned the practice of having a ton of 2,000 pounds for coke, 2,240 pounds for anthracite coal, 2,268 pounds for pig iron, and 2,464 pounds for blooms. This was discussed by Mr. Warner, (Ala.,) Hough, Patterson, Coffin, Martin, Eifurt, and Seidel.

Mr. Milnes offered the following resolution, which was agreed to:

Resolved, That a committee of five be appointed by the Chair to take into consideration the matter of the adoption of a uniform ton of 2,000 pounds in all transactions in iron, and of the adoption of a uniform standard of measure and weight for charcoal; and that said committee be instructed to report at the next meeting; also, that the committee be instructed to request the coöperation of all iron workers and dealers in the United States.

The President announced that the membership had increased in some States to such an extent, as to entitle them to additional members on the Board of Managers, and stated that the following names had been presented: Horace Magee, West Virginia; R. L. Martin, Pennsylvania; W. H. H. Gere, New York; and M. Hoagland, New Jersey. They were elected by acclamation additional members of the Board.

The Executive Committee presented to the Association the name of Mr. J. C. Bayles, editor of the "Iron Age," as an honorary and corresponding member. The Association unanimously adopted the recommendation of the committee.

The proposed answer to the telegram of Mr. Fuller was read and approved, and the Secretary directed to send it as read.

Mr. A. G. Curtin, junior, of Pennsylvania, presented the following resolutions; which were unanimously adopted:

WHEREAS, The visiting members of the United States Association of Charcoal Iron Workers, feeling a deep sense of obligation for the many attentions and favors shown them, desire to give expression to their gratitude in shape to admit of its incorporation with our permanent records; be it

Resolved, That we are deeply indebted to the Manufacturers of Harrisburg, for the elegant banquet tendered us, and to Colonel G. B. Wiestling and Mr. J. C. Fuller, for hospitable and generous entertainment at their respective furnaces.

That we heartily thank the officers of the Philadelphia and Reading railroad, the Pennsylvania railroad, the Cumberland Valley railroad, the Mont Alto railroad, the South Mountain railroad, and the Cornwall railroad, for unusual courtesies which have added so much to the pleasure of our excursions.

That we thank the proprietors of the Central Iron Works, Chesapeake Nail Works, and Paxton Rolling Mills, the Harrisburg Car Manufacturing Company, the Wister Furnace, the Pennsylvania Steel Works, the Perry Forge, and the Cornwall Ore Bank Company, for the courtesy and freedom with which they have opened their works and mines to inspection, and for the polite attention shown us.

That we are under great obligations to the local committees in Harrisburg, Chambersburg, and Lebanon, for having secured us so warm a welcome, and for the excellent provision they have made for our comfort in every way. Also to the Young Men's Christian Association, of Harrisburg, for the use of their elegant hall.

Resolved, That the Secretary be authorized to convey the substance of these resolutions to the gentlemen and companies named, and to all others who have favored us, with the assurance that our expression of thanks in this case is something more than the perfunctory discharge of a formal duty—an honest utterance which but feebly expresses our real feeling.

Resolved, That the Harrisburg meeting is "a success" in every respect, and that we shall always remember it with pleasure and profit, for the information gained, the hospitalities enjoyed, the new acquaintances made, and the old friendships cemented.

Mr. Milnes offered the following; which was adopted:

WHEREAS, It is fitting at this meeting to express our acknowledgements to those whose faithful and zealous service in organizing and conducting our affairs, has made, this association what it is.

Resolved, That our thanks are especially due to our Secretary, Mr. John Birkinbine, for his earnest labors to promote the interests of the United States Association of Charcoal Iron Workers, and for the able and conscientious manner in which he has discharged the labors and responsibilities of his office. Also, to our President and Board of Managers, for what they have done in laying the foundations of our future usefulness.

Mr. Coffin expressed the thanks of the Association to the ladies who had graced the meetings, and added to the pleasure of the excursions by their presence.

A paper from Mr. Alfred L. Tyler, of Alabama, was read by the Secretary, entitled "Notes on Furnaces in Alabama."

The Association directed that, for want of time to read them, a lengthy and valuable paper, sent to the Secretary by Mr. N. Lilienberg, on "Building and working of blast furnaces in Sweden," and, also, paper on "charcoal transportation," by the Secretary, be published in the "Journal." (These will appear in future issues.)

The Secretary made a few remarks on the progress and prospects of charcoal iron making.

Hon. Willard Warner, of Alabama, in remarks to the Association, urged upon the members the importance of each one feeling himself to be a committee of one to work for the building up of the Association, until every charcoal furnace and forge in the United States is represented; and to further work for the attainment of the purposes of the Association until it was first-class in every particular, and recognized the world over as authority in its particular branch of iron industry.

The remarks of Mr. Warner were heartily indorsed by Mr. C. E. Coffin, of Maryland.

Adjourned.

Narrative of the Annual Meeting.

Our only regret in connection with the Harrisburg meeting is that more of the charcoal iron workers of the country could not arrange their business to unite with us. We, however, congratulate the Association on the attendance and on the large portion of the United States which was represented.

The headquarters of the Executive Committee, in the Lochiel Hotel, was sought by the members as they arrived, and mutual introductions speedily followed, so that by the time the initial session was called to order, Tuesday evening, all felt at home.

After formal adjournment, the members of the Association were escorted to the Lochiel Hotel, where a banquet was tendered by the business men of Harrisburg. When those invited had assembled, Mr. William T. Hildrup, on behalf of the manufacturers of Harrisburg, welcomed the Association to the city in the following words:

GENTLEMEN OF THE UNITED STATES ASSOCIATION OF CHARCOAL IRON WORKERS: It has been assigned to me to give you words of welcome from the business interests of this city. You have been welcomed to our city by His Honor, the Mayor—an honest, earnest welcome, fittingly spoken and sincerely entertained. It is eminently fitting that the business interests and people greet you with respectful welcome, that fellow crafts extend their greetings. Hat in hand, as respectful juniors, you are the representatives of one of the oldest industries known to man. Prehistoric legends extend charcoal workings of iron back thousands of years beyond the Christian era. The Greeks claim to have been taught it by special favor of the gods as early as 1432 B. C., by sending down the lightning to burn the forests, thus smelting the ore, and leaving the product pure iron. Moses extends its discovery back 2,000 years before his time; and you are to-day the representatives of the ancient method charcoal iron workers. We who represent railroads, with their many and diversified interests, telegraphs, cotton factories, and anthracite iron industries, are infants among you. The working of iron by stone coal and coke, discovered 250 years ago, is a mere infant by your side, and anthracite furnaces, like mushrooms, are a thing of a night and a day. What is more to the point, while the wheels of time go round, and you grow hoary with honored age, you have maintained character for excellence, and all bow to the fact that you make the best iron, [loud applause,]—that your ancient character for excellence has not been contaminated by new fashions or by new-fangled notions.

Gentlemen, although you are venerable in age, superior in excellence, you yet bear the palm of progressing with the times, improving in methods, increasing products, economizing costs, mixing brains with charcoal, showing that you have your share of the best progressive men with you. While representing antiquity, you have a perpetual fountain of youth supplying your ranks with energy, skill, industry, linked with inventing and improving ingenuity.

The chapters of all your worth and excellencies are not to be told in brevity. We may passingly hint at them, to show our esteem, and the warmth of our welcome which we extend to you on this occasion. [Applause.]

Hon. William Milnes, Jr., of Virginia, briefly returned the thanks of the Association for the cordial welcome; after which the large gathering sat down to and partook of the sumptuous collation.

Then followed a series of toasts, which brought out many witty and bright sayings from the members, our guests, and the local committee of Harrisburg.

The following gentlemen kindly served as a local committee at Harrisburg, who, besides providing the banquet and securing the gratuitous use of the Young Men's Christian Association hall for our meetings, left nothing undone to secure our comfort and gratification during the progress of the meeting: Hon. Henry M. Hoyt, Hon. Charles L. Bailey, Henry McCormick, L. S. Bent, Abraham S. Patterson, Joseph H. Landis, John Q. Denny, Henry Seidle, W. W. Jennings, G. Russell Lincoln, James Boyd, S. M. Prevost, Spencer C. Gilbert, W. T. Hildrup, Hon. J. D. Patterson, Jones Wister, Henry Gilbert, Lane S. Hart, S. L. Chauvenet, James A. Clark, Luther D. Jauss, Andrew S. McCreath, Thomas L. Wallace, H. B. Beatty, John B. McPherson, R. L. Muench, H. B. Mitchell, G. M. McCauley.

At 8.30, Wednesday morning, a special train, generously provided by the Cumberland Valley Railroad Company, steamed out of Harrisburg with our party, numbering seventy-five, and, crossing the Susquehanna river, carried us rapidly up the Cumberland Valley 18 miles, to the outskirts of Carlisle, the junction of the South Mountain railroad.

For 19 miles we traveled on the South Mountain railroad, passing up the valley of Mountain Creek, through hills thickly wooded, to the property of the South Mountain Mining and Iron Company, of which Mr. J. C. Fuller (who was pleasantly called "the Father of the Association," on account of his exertions for its establishment) is president.

This company owns the railroad, a tract of 27,000 acres, several large farms, a forge, a furnace, and a number of ore banks.

The first stop made was at Laurel Ore Bank, which is in condition for immediate work. From there the forge near by was visited. This is an old plant, and consists of 6 forge fires and 4 tuyere run-out fire. Blast is supplied by two iron blowing cylinders, 40 inches in diameter and 4 feet stroke, operated by a 24 foot over-shot water-wheel. The loops are wrought under a cast-iron helve hammer, lifted by a cam in front, which receives motion from a 15 foot under-shot water-wheel.

From the forge the party was taken, by cars, two miles to the old Pine Grove ore bank, (now producing 70 to 100 tons of ore per day,) which exhibited some remarkable faces of excellent ore. This bank had at one time been abandoned, and filled with water, but from present indications a supply can be obtained from it for many years to come. It appears inexhaustible.

The furnace, which is close by the ore bank, is a stone stack, 32 feet high; and iron casing, 14 feet high. The total height, therefore, is 44 feet.

The bosh is 9 feet 4 inches diameter. The crucible 50 inches diameter. The furnace is blown with 3 tuyeres. Has water-dam and tymp, and is furnished with sunken bell and hopper, to secure center drop. An 18 pipe hot-blast stove heats the blast, and two double boilers, 36 inches in diameter, and 30 feet long, supply steam to a vertical Weimer engine, with blowing tub 5 feet in diameter, and 2 feet stroke. This engine was in the Machinery Hall of the Centennial Exhibition. The stock-house is provided with a steam hoisting engine and railroad tracks on trestles, making convenient bins for receiving materials. A neat brick engine and casting-houses add to the appearance of the plant. After inspecting the works, the mansion, and the village, the party were escorted to Pine Grove Park, where a substantial luncheon was spread, to which all did full justice. The train was then taken for South Mountain Junction, passing a succession of valuable hematite ore mines en route.

The excursionists are indebted to Mr. W. H. Woodward, Superintendent of the railroad, for courtesies extended, he having accompanied the party while on his road.

Iron has been made at Pine Grove since 1770. The specialty

of the furnace is forge-pig, which is made into blooms at the company's "Laurel" forge and other forges, for the manufacture of flange and fire-box plate iron. At present the furnace is making about 100 tons pig iron per week.

After leaving South Mountain Junction, and passing through the historic town of Carlisle, the train carried us 34 miles further up the Cumberland Valley to Chambersburg, where Colonel T. B. Kennedy, President, and General J. F. Boyd, Superintendent of the Cumberland Valley railroad, with the following Committe on Reception, met the party: Major John Stevenson, D. S. Hunter, Honorable John Sweeny, Levi Springer, C. Burkhart.

Before going to the various hotels, the "Falling Spring" furnace, close by the depot, was visited. This is a new plant, and consists of a stack 9 feet bosh by 40 feet high, encased in a sheet-iron shell, resting upon iron columns. It is provided with bell and hopper, has water tymp and dam, and is blown with one tuyere at present. The furnace is making 10 tons of car-wheel iron per day; it has a stone hearth, and fire-brick in-wall.

Blast is supplied by a vertical Weimer engine, with blowing cylinder 40 inches diameter, and 20 inches stroke. A belt attached to the fly-wheel operates the hoist. A crusher is run by a separate engine. Steam is furnished by 3 boilers, operating steam mill, and furnace, and crusher.

A feature of the plant is, that it is run in connection with a large flour-mill of C. Burkhart & Co., who also own the furnace. The waste gases from the tunnel-head, (the furnace uses cold blast,) being utilized for generating steam to operate the mill.

The ladies, generally, remained in their hotel in the evening, but a fair audience gathered in the court-house, and listened to Judge Rowe's able address of welcome, and to the papers read.

Thursday morning at eight o'clock, our special train was ready, and bidding adieu to Chambersburg, we were taken a few miles back towards Harrisburg, and there switched off on the Mont Alto railroad, which extends to Waynesboro', 19 miles distant. This road, in connection with the property of the Mont Alto Iron Company, is under the management of Colonel George B. Wiestling, President of our organization, who, with his brother, Mr. Edw. B. Wiestling, made the excursionists feel greatly at home.

After a short stop at Pond Ore Bank, the train carried us to the furnace and forge, which are adjacent to each other. Here Hon. Fred'k Watts, late United States Commissioner of Agriculture, and a veteran charcoal iron-worker, joined the party. The Mont Alto estate consists of 20,200 acres, 1,000 acres of which are under cultivation, divided into seven farms. The furnace is quite ancient looking, but the forge is modern in all its arrangements. The furnace is 9 feet 6 inches diameter at bosh, and 36 feet high; it is open top, with covering lid, and is blown with three tuyeres into a crucible 54 inches in diameter. The furnace has neither dam nor tymp, two holes in the fire-brick work serving as tapping hole and cinder notch.

Blast is furnished by two iron blowing cylinders, 46 inches diameter and six feet stroke, driven by a horizental steam engine, 18 inches diameter cylinder by 4 feet stroke. A small hot-blast stove, containing 32 pipes, 3 inches bore, heats the blast, and three flue boilers, 3 feet diameter and 24 feet long, furnish steam for the engine.

The cinder is all granulated in water and raised by elevator buckets into bins, from which it flows into carts or cars. As this is a bank furnace, no hoist is required, and the ore, flux, and fuel is hauled to the bridge house by wagon. A portion of the coal is brought by wagon beds, which are transferred from the running gear on to railroad cars and then to running gears again.

The furnace is now making 16 tons of iron per day, the product being sold for car wheel purposes, or made into blooms, for flange plate, and fire-box iron, at the forge.

Blast for the run-out and forge is supplied by two blast cylinders, three feet diameter by four feet stroke, driven by a horizontal steam engine, 12″x24″ stroke, supplied with steam from a fire-box boiler, located over the run-out fire, and utilizing its otherwise waste heat.

The run out is a double furnace, with four tuyeres. The forge has 8 sinking fires, which heat a cylinder boiler, 33 inches diameter by 38 feet long, generating steam for a Nasmith steam hammer, with a two-ton ram, under which the blooms are wrought.

There are three distinct belts of brown hematite iron ore on the property, on which there are twenty separate openings, or mines, five of which are now being worked, furnishing, besides the entire amount used by the furnace, a considerable for consumption in the Susquehanna and Lehigh districts. Two of these mines are underground workings, and the balance are open. Five limestone quarries on the estate are available for flux, and the stone is broken to uniform size in a Blake crusher. Iron was first made at Mont Alto in 1808. A chafery, merchant bar-mill, and nail works were at one time part of the plant, but have not been in operation since 1866.

There are, also, near the forge, five charcoal kilns of various sizes and forms, some coal hearths, and an iron retort, where the Manager made some interesting experiments upon the value of coaling in kilns or heaps, and also for utilizing the acetic vapors from wood distillation. We shall publish the results in the discussion of the paper "Our Fuels," in a future issue of the Journal.

A short walk from the furnace brought the party to Mont Alto park, where a substantial luncheon, embracing every requisite, even to hot bricks, was prepared. After partaking of lunch, and returning thanks, the cars were boarded, and the party returned to Harrisburg.

The two parks, Pine Grove and Mont Alto, are features which were very pleasing. They are both replete with rustic structures, and every convenience for the large number of pic-nic parties which yearly travel over the respective railroads. They are widely different in arrangements, and were both hugely enjoyed.

Arriving at Harrisburg, a special train, under the personal charge of Mr. S. M. Prevost, Superintendent of the Middle Division of the Pennsylvania railroad, (furnished by the courtesy of the company,) was in waiting. After embarking, we were taken to the Chesapeake Nail Works, of Charles L. Bailey & Co., where the proprietors personally explained the various processes of puddling, heating, rolling, nail-cutting, cleaning, blueing, and packing, at the rate of 4,000 kegs of nails per week.

Passing thence into the Central Iron Works, controlled by the same firm, the magnificent plant of 3 high chilled rolls, 96 inches long and 31 inches in diameter, (made of charcoal iron,) was seen at work, rolling boiler-plates from charcoal blooms. This mill produces 7,000 tons boiler-plate and tank iron annually.

The next point visited was the Paxton furnaces and plate mills. These mills were also rolling charcoal blooms into plate iron. There are two blast furnaces here, the larger being 16 feet diameter of bosh, and 60 feet high, blown with 5 tuyeres, the blast being heated in 3 Whitwell hot-blast stoves, each 18 feet diameter, and 60 feet high, the fuel being ½ coke and ½ anthracite coal. The smaller furnace is 14 feet diameter at bosh, 50 feet high, blown with 6 tuyeres, the blast being heated in one cast-iron pipe stove, with 60 pipes, 8″×14′. The fuel is ¼ coke and ¾ anthracite coal. Blast is furnished by two horizontal steam blowing engines, and one beam engine.

The larger furnace is making 60 tons of Bessemer pig per day, on ores averaging 50 per cent. The smaller, the 30 tons of pig per day, on a mixture yielding 42 per cent. of iron in the furnace.

The last visit of the day was made to the Wister furnace, a stone stack built in 1867. It has a bosh of 14 feet, and is 45 feet high, blown with 5 tuyeres, the blast being heated in two iron-pipe stoves, of Kent pattern, one 40 and one 50 pipes. A horizontal engine, 30 inches×4feet, driving two horizontal blowing tubs, each 6 feet×6 feet, furnishes the blast.

The furnace labors under the disadvantage of being low, but makes 245 tons to 275 tons of mill iron per week, with ores averaging 50 per cent. A point of interest at the Wister furnace, was the kilns for roasting sulphurous ores.

This furnace, considering its disadvantages, has maintained a most excellent record, both for quantity and quality of product.

The final session, on Thursday evening, in the Young Men's Christian Association hall, Harrisburg, was notable for the very able paper by Professor Hough. It closed with the resolutions of thanks given in our minutes.

Eight o'clock, Friday morning, found the party on a special train of the Pennsylvania railroad, which carried us 6 miles up the Susquehanna river, to the gap in the Blue Mountains, and across the iron bridge, which was constructed in the place of a wooden one, without stopping a train. The foggy weather interfered with the view of the gap, and was our only disappointment during the excursion.

Arriving at Marysville, Seidel Bros.' Perry Forge was inspected, and Mr. J. B. Seidel, a veteran charcoal iron worker, father of the proprietors, assisted his sons in showing us the works.

This property is located convenient to a large timber supply, and close to the railroad and river. It consists of a six tuyere run-out fire, six single tuyere forge fires, and a wooden helve hammer, raised by cam at the nose.

Blast is furnished by a Baker blower, driven by a 12×20 steam engine; while the hammer is operated by power transmitted by belt from a high-breast water-wheel. The boiler is fired with bituminous coal.

The forge uses both charcoal and anthracite iron, as the orders received demand, and has made 210 net tons per month.

From Marysville, the train returned to Harrisburg, and stopped at the works of the Harrisburg Car Manufacturing Company, where piles of various charcoal irons, aggregating 2,500 tons, were examined, and the process of making car wheels was inspected. We contemplate publishing shortly some data on car wheels and car wheel irons, which will embody the experience of Mr. W. T. Hildrup, manager of these works.

The works cover an area of 6 acres, employ 800 men, and can turn out 12 eight-wheeled box-cars per day.

The capacity of the car wheel department is 130 per day, made from charcoal pig-iron and old car wheels.

Passing through Harrisburg, the works of the Pennsylvania Steel Company, at Steelton, three miles below, were visited, and two hours were spent in examining this immense plant.

The property embraces 120 acres. There are two blast furnaces in operation, and two more building. The present furnaces are No. 1, 60×14 feet, with iron pipe hot blast stoves; and No. 2, 77×17 feet 6 inches, with Whitwell stoves.

These furnaces produce 900 tons of pig iron per week, and the new furnaces, which are to measure 60×16, will increase this capacity to 1,900 tons per week.

The Bessemer plant consists of two 5-ton converters, which transform 9,000 to 10,000 tons of pig-iron per month into steel ingots.

Three additional converters are being erected, which will augment the capacity of the Bessemer plant to 2,000 tons per month.

Two open hearth steel furnaces produce 300 tons of ingots per week from pig iron, steel scrap, and iron ore, and an addition of two more furnaces will increase the output to 6,000 tons per month.

From the Bessemer and open-hearth plants, the ingots are taken hot to regenerative furnaces, and given a wash-heat. They then pass through a three-high train of blooming rolls, and are cut under an 8-ton hammer into blooms. These blooms are reheated in regenerative furnaces, passed through 3-high roughing and finishing trains, and come out finished rails, which, after being cut to length and straightened, pass on to the cooling tables.

The present mills can make 410 tons of steel rails per day.

The extensive machine-shop and foundry connected with the works manufactures all the machinery required about the plant.

The company make a specialty of heavy steel forgings, which are wrought under a 15-ton steam hammer, and of steel billets for various purposes. Also a 4-ton hammer for light forgings.

One large building is devoted to the manufacture of railroad frogs, crossings, and switches.

The present stock of material on hand for the furnaces comprises 50,000 tons of foreign and domestic ores; 5,000 tons of coal and coke; and there is pig iron on hand to the amount of 35,000 tons, 25,000 of which was imported from England during the "boom."

Major Bent, the superintendent, and his corps of assistants, accompanied the visitors through the works, and courteously explained all the details.

A tour through a plant of such magnitude was calculated to dwarf our individual enterprises in our estimation, but it was replete in instructive features, and demonstrated the necessity of economies in handling by the employment of labor-saving appliances wherever possible; and showed the practical benefit of continuous processes, both of which can be utilized more than they now are in the charcoal iron industry.

Returning to the Lochiel hotel for dinner, we started on our final excursion, the Philadelphia and Reading railroad (through the courtesy of Mr. F. B. Gowen) having kindly provided two special cars on the afternoon express, for Lebanon, 26 miles distant. Here Mr. A. Wilhelm, manager of the immense estates at Cornwall, met us, with a number of prominent citizens of Lebanon. An engine of the Cornwall railroad was attached to our cars, and, before we had finished our introductions, we were at Cornwall. Here an unusual favor was extended. Our cars were pushed up the spiral railway, which twice encircles the big hill, rising at the rate of 200 feet per mile. Alighting, the summit was soon reached, and the excursionists divided their exclamations of gratification between the wonderful exhibit of mineral in sight and the magnificent panorama of the rich agricultural valley, extending for many miles. Behind us was the same South Mountain range, which had been examined 60 miles away, at Pine Grove and Mont Alto. Twenty miles in front was the North or Blue Mountain, whilst between the two ranges lay the beautiful Lebanon valley, with the town of Lebanon and its seven anthracite blast furnaces.

Closer to us were the mansions of the estate and the 6 anthracite furnaces at Cornwall; the old charcoal furnace was just at the foot of the hill.

Of the ore and the immensity of the deposit, we can scarcely write so as to give our members who were not with us an idea. Standing on the summit of the "big hill," we saw an immense dike of magnetic ore, averaging 500 to 600 feet in width, bounded by trap, and extending through the "big hill," "middle hill," and "grassy hill" for about 4,000 feet in length.

The point on which we stood was 365 feet above the little stream which separated the "big and middle hills." The latter is 225 feet, and the grassy hill 175 feet above the creek level.

The dyke is ALL ORE; the railroad tracks are laid on ore; the wharves from which the cars are loaded are of ore; and immense faces of exposed ore demonstrate that the value of these hills, which once were sold for a few hundred dollars, can only be represented now by many millions of dollars. Estimates of the quantity of ore in these hills above the creek level have varied from 40 to 60 million tons, and diamond drill explorations have shown the deposit to extend far below that level.

The ore is a sulphurous magnetite, averaging in the blast furnace 50 per cent. of metallic iron, and occasional nests or veins of red oxide and sulphuret of copper are found. Some remarkable specimens of "lode-stone" have been taken from the hills.

Passing down the spiral railroad, the train next made the circuit of the "middle hill," and stopped at the Bird Coleman furnaces, where an opportunity of inspecting the furnace in blast, and the one now building, was given. A peculiarity of the operation of the Cornwall furnaces is that cinder is held until it is above the tuyeres, being kept back from them by the strong blast employed; and, when tapped, a large opening permits the discharge of any bone, slate, or foreign material, with the cinder, which passes out in a large stream. While at the furnace, cinder was flushed, and a cast of iron made. The visit to Cornwall closed with an inspection of the old charcoal furnace, which is a brownstone stack, blown with cold blast, through 2 tuyeres, the blast being supplied by two wooden double-acting blowing tubs, operated by a high-pressure horizontal steam engine, through gearing on what was formerly the rim of the water-wheel, giving motion to the tubs. The boiler is placed at the tunnel head. The furnace is 31 feet high, and 8 feet bosh.

There are two rectangular 80-cord kilns at the furnace.

One item of interest to the excursionists was that this cold blast furnace has been running a lengthy campaign on a fire-brick hearth.

Before leaving Cornwall, Col. Wiestling thanked the hosts for their kindness, and three cheers attested the hearty second of the excursionists. After a generous invitation from General Warner to the Association to hold its next meeting in the South, the train returned to Lebanon, where supper was spread in the Lebanon Valley House, which was relished by all, after the exercise at Cornwall.

Here the separations began, but those who returned in the special cars to Harrisburg found a pleasant surprise in store in an informal reception given them by Mr. and Mrs. Charles L. Bailey.

Thus ended a most successful and enjoyable meeting, free from disappointments, and full of instruction to all who attended. We have done our best to give those who were not with us an idea of what we learned, and preserve in our annals a memorial of *a good time.*

Address delivered before the United States Association of Charcoal Iron Workers, at its Annual Session.

By GEO. B. WIESTLING, *President.*

ASSOCIATE CHARCOAL IRON WORKERS:

Whatever interest may attach to the history of our organization, its date is too recent, and the circumstances attending it too familiar to all, to warrant me in consuming your time by referring to it in any other than a general way. When we consider that the date of the first use of charcoal for metallurgical purposes is so remote as to have been lost in the obscurity of past ages; when we reflect upon the magnitude of the interests involved; upon the large quantities of raw stock that have been consumed; the many streams that were harnessed in the work long before we have any record of the practical use of steam; yea, that manual labor not only prepared the fuel, and transported it, mined the ore, quarried the limestone, and conducted the process, but also furnished the power by which the blast was supplied; that the thought, anxiety, and care incident to every department of preparation and manufacture, for so many years have burdened the brain and body of man; it seems strange that, so far as we know, it devolved upon the charcoal iron masters of the present day to first associate themselves together to reason, compare, discuss; to procure and furnish statistics; "to provide for the mutual interchange of practical and scientific knowledge and experience; and to take proper measures for advancing and protecting the trade in all its branches."

This may be largely attributable to the lack of communication and transportation facilities under which our predecessors labored, and to the superior advantages and opportunities which we enjoy. But be this as it may, to greater facilities and larger opportunities attach proportional responsibilities; and our duty to ourselves, our obligations to our fellow-men, and a proper legacy of information to those who will fill our places after our labor is ended, required that we should use the means at hand to perfect our knowledge; to increase and improve our products; to endeavor to fathom and elucidate what may have seemed mysterious and incomprehensible; to keep fully apace with our compeers in other branches of metallurgy; to care for and economize the bounties of nature, and to hand down to posterity a record stamped with the impress of work well done. Influenced by these views, we were prompted to assemble for consultation, and the result appeared in the organization of the United States Association of Charcoal Iron Workers. The responsibilities were not assumed, for they already rested upon us.

It was accountability which confronted us, and still demands its tribute; and now, at the close of the first year of our organized existence, as we come together at our annual gathering, from near and distant parts of our common country, the magnitude of our undertaking is undiminished; the responsibilities still challenge our best efforts; and these only stimulate us in our determination to move forward to success.

The Executive Committee congratulates you that the efforts of the past fiscal year have strengthened our foundations, and developed our inherent power for good. We have communicated, through our Secretary, with almost all, if not every, the Charcoal Iron works in the United States.

We have increased our membership, and obtained valuable statistics and information. We have established our Journal, and issued two numbers. And we expect, at this annual meeting, to gather a rich harvest from the seed sown.

A report of receipts and expenditures will be submitted by our Treasurer, from which it will be seen that any more vigorous development of our aims were circumscribed by the limits of our *finances*.

The provisions of our Constitution contemplate the enlistment and coöperation of every person practically engaged or interested, by reason of capital invested, in any process of charcoal iron production, and we look for the active agency of every present member to secure this end.

Our field is extensive enough to satisfy the most ambitious, varied enough to gratify the tastes or particular forte of every member, and important enough to enlist the energies of every charcoal iron worker.

The subject of forrestry affects directly our own interests, and alike the interest of every resident of the habitable globe, while proper fence, cattle, and road laws are not only important to us, but are sure indices of the advanced civilization of the day.

The subjects which demand our attention are so varied and numerous, that one is almost bewildered in their contemplation. The preservation and cultivation of timber, the economical chopping and cording of wood, and its transportation; the manufacture of different kinds of charcoal, in meilers, kilns, and retorts; the utilization of waste products in charring; the transportation of charcoal, its storage, and its economical use in the different manufacturing processes; the proper and complete analyses of ores and limestones; the mining of ores and quarrying of limestone; the condition of labor, and the well-being of the communities dependent upon us; the process; the plant; the product, and the financial result.

I pause in the list, not from an exhaustion of topics, for you well know what an amount of detail is involved in each department, and how minute the sub-divisions of each item may be. And I ask your attention for a few moments, to the necessarily brief consideration of a few thoughts on some of our manufacturing processes, and the resultant products.

First, the blast furnace. An examination of the many different shapes and widely differing lines of charcoal blast furnaces, would lead a casual observer to conclude that the lines and proportions were of but little consequence, and that the iron could be successfully made in a construction of any shape or kind.

Open top furnaces exhibit tunnel heads from one sixth up to one half the diameter of boshes; hearths are rectangular, oval, or circular; large and small forehearths, and closed fronts are used; heavy buck walls are still in existence, while some hearths are made thin, with a single length of furnace block, and void of all casing or backing.

But the greatest variation is probably in the inclination of the boshes. Surely all cannot be right, and we even doubt if the plea of existing local circumstances, could be successfully maintained in justification.

It is well known that water may be boiled in the shell of an egg, or, if you please, under proper conditions, in a paper box, and yet this fact that it is possible, does not indorse vessels of this character for the purpose, nor prompt us to use them.

Possibly, a careful study of our plants might awaken the suspicion that we are using metallurgical "paper boxes." We know of charcoal furnace boshes inclining over 45°, or more than one foot horizontal, to one foot vertical, and others one and a half inches horizontal to one foot vertical.

A metallurgical work, which probably has a place in the library of the majority of charcoal iron masters, in referring to the boshes of furnaces, lays down the rule, that the more friable the fuel, the steeper the bosh should be, and alleges that hence coke furnaces have steeper boshes than anthracite plants. But what becomes of this logic, when the same authority offers a model charcoal furnace in which the boshes, with this *most friable* fuel, are flatter than even anthracite? It is plainly inconsistent.

Experience has established that boshes for coke *should* be steeper than for anthracite. But is it not on account of the greater coherence of coke? And should not the inclination of the boshes be strongly dependent upon the relative angle of repose of different fuels? I do not believe that the friability of the fuel has anything to do with the inclination of boshes. If it has, then charcoal being more friable than either anthracite or coke, would require steeper boshes than either. I *do* believe that the relative cohesion of the fuel should have a marked influence on the lines. If so, then what relation should charcoal boshes have to those of other fuels? Has it greater or less cohesion? Is its angle of repose greater or less? A simple, practical experiment bearing on this was tried with cold fuel at Mont Alto. A charcoal wagon, with given batter of sides and ends, was first loaded with anthracite coal, and hauled around to effectually settle the load. The bottom boards were drawn, and the load promptly discharged itself. This was the anticipated result.

The same bed was then loaded with coke, and under the same conditions, the bottom boards were drawn. The discharge was not near so prompt or rapid as with anthracite, because the pieces of coke stuck together, or cohered, to a greater extent, but the load entirely emptied itself from the bed. Then the same bed was loaded with charcoal, in the same condition as that charged into the furnace, and, after properly settling the load, the bottom boards were again drawn.

The result in this case every member knows. The load did *not* promptly discharge, but it was necessary to shake the bed and compel the charcoal to fall from it.

Probably the relative cohesion should be determined when the fuels are incandescent, but the result, under the conditions, certainly appears to advise steeper boshes than with either anthracite or coke. Flat boshes, forming acute angles with the in-walls, certainly encourage and promote scaffolding and funneling, with all their train of ills; and *that* inclination, or those lines which offer the most impediment to the gradual, uniform, continuous descent of stock, or which tends to provoke lodgments, scaffolds, and bridges, is surely the most remote from the best. The progress made in the sciences seems more or less unfortunate for some persons, in that it robs us of excellent scapegoats for our ignorance. How prone men have been, and still are, to attribute anything beyond their immediate comprehension to something mysterious; to electricity; or to some peculiar, not exactly understood, chemical combination. It is like placing the fault on the absent one.

It is not a very long time ago, since the longest campaign on record of a charcoal furnace was fifteen months, and the average was under nine months, and the accepted reason was, that charcoal had some mysterious chemical effect upon the hearth, destroying it much more rapidly than would either coke, raw coal, or anthracite. This has all been dissipated, and campaigns can be made, and are being made, with charcoal furnaces, extending over periods of six years, and there is no reason why the operation cannot be much further prolonged.

The popular impression is, that charcoal furnaces are necessarily insignificant affairs at best, and their capacity for output very limited. But the fact is that a greater quantity of iron per cubical foot of furnace is attainable with charcoal than with any other fuel. So, also, with reference to the materials composing the hearth, the question often asked, whether fire-brick would answer for charcoal furnaces, has been, in my judgment, practically demonstrated. The same mystery has attached to the product of charcoal blast furnaces. Why should the quality of charcoal iron be superior to iron made with other fuel? It is simply obedient to the law that every seed bringeth forth after its kind, and being free from the impurities which attach to other fuels, its product is proportionally pure. But let us not forget that impurities, robbing the product of its deservedly good reputation, may be introduced through the ore and flux. And now, before leaving charcoal pig iron, I cannot refrain from some allusion to the unsolved mystery of its chilling properties. From time immemorial, this property has been supposed to have been entirely monopolized by charcoal iron.

The hidden secret, as though not shrouded in sufficient gloom, is further obscured by being pronounced by consumers to be dependent upon the low temperature of the blast, and this view is still largely entertained, and the alchemist in the recesses of his laboratory labors in vain to solve the problem. This solution, however intricate, certainly devolves upon this association, or at least we should make an honest effort to clear away the mists which surround the question.

We grade our irons from grey to white, from soft to hard, and may not chilling iron really be a grade? The grade being largely the result of the temperature of the furnace, may not chilling iron depend more upon furnace temperature, and not upon that of the blast? This is more or less substantiated by the fact that Salisbury, Baltimore, Muirkirk, and other car-wheel irons of unquestioned repute, are all made with hot blast, and would seem to demonstrate that whatever temperature of blast, renders the work of the furnace most controllable and uniform; that will enable the manager to hold longest continuously on any one grade is proper and best in making car-wheel or chilling iron. We know that some impurities tend to an easier make of close or high iron, and also of that grade which chills and yet is grey;

but in general the temperature of the furnace establishes the grade. If this be true, then charcoal iron does *not monopolize* chilling properties, as has been hitherto supposed. The charcoal carries no subtle substance into the iron that improves its quality. Its beauty and value lies in the fact that it carries no evil, no impurity with it to injure the iron. And may it not be that the hitherto accepted dogma is untenable, and that charcoal carries nothing with it to cause iron to chill, neither will its purity help the chilling property, for impurities may be more effective. The expression of this view may be considered as tending more to benefit the anthracite and coke iron branch than the charcoal. But we are searchers after truth and must accept its teachings. Something more than mere chilling property is requisite for car-wheels. The iron must possess that strength and elasticity which results from pure stock; and so long as the charcoal iron master uses ores and fluxes, which will favorably compare with their pure fuel, they will monopolize the car-wheel trade, and so long as charcoal pig iron, possessing chilling properties, and exhibiting a tensile strength of forty-one thousand pounds per square inch, can be made with *hot blast*, the theory that the low temperature of the blast effects either the strength or the chill of iron, needs, in my estimation, further verifying evidence.

The run-out fire is probably the best abused of all the furnaces in use. Condemned for extravagance and accused of uselessness, it is as little, if not less, understood than any portion of a plant, and, under proper construction and management, it may yet prove at least as good a dephosphorizing process as some others that are commended.

It is not many years since, when quality was the essential point in iron, that every puddling furnace, even in rail mills, was supplied with stock that had passed through a run out. It was never abandoned because it made the iron superior, but because it made it too expensive, and it and other desirable features were abandoned or omitted in deference to cheapness.

Now, both steel and iron processes seek for an intermediate dephosphorizing, purifying process, to occupy the ground which the run out held, and still partially holds, though largely regarded with contempt.

Do we understand our run outs? If so, why is their manipulation vested in certain families of workmen, and the detail of their operation magnified and made mysterious? Why do run-out men, as a rule, use one kind of flux, viz: forge cinder only, without any reference to the iron they are working, and we assent to it? Why do we persist in the use of siliceous bottoms? Why do we not tap off the cinder when it is ladened with the impurities, and before they again combine with the iron, and bathe the molten metal with fresh basic flux? To what extent does the run out, even as now used, eliminate impurities? Probably when we understand and use the fire as we should, we will feel like respecting it more.

In an excellent article on the "Run-out Fire," contained in the last number of our Journal, speaking of its purifying effects, we are presented with a partial analysis of ore, pig iron, run-out metal, run-out and forge cinder.

It is to be regretted that the analysis is not full and complete, but it shows that all the phosphorus contained in the ore, combined in the blast furnace with the iron, and that in the run-out fire, eighty per cent. of the silicon, and sixty per cent. of the phosphorous, were eliminated from the pig iron. What kind of a bottom, and what flux was used, is not stated. I desire, however, to take exception, courteously and kindly, to one statement in the article, which the Editor of the JOURNAL gave as he received it, and which reads thus: "The ore had a tendency to be "cold short, but the coke used in the run-out fire parted with "some of its sulphur, which passed into the run-out metal, from "which a neutral bloom was made." This assumes that sulphur, which makes iron red short, will form a chemical combination with phosphorus, which makes iron cold short, and that thus the effects of one or both are neutralized, leaving the iron neutral, *i. e.*, neither red nor cold short.

The correctness of this assumption I entirely doubt. If it was true, the disposition of these two baneful impurities would be quite simple. It would only be necessary to use a sulphurous limestone, with a cold short ore in the blast furnace, and to smelt with a sulphurous coke, and *vice versa*. A certain percentage of phosphorus is necessary to develop the cold short property in iron, and for the present, let us assume this quantity to be one half of one per cent. For the sake of the argument, let us also assume that one sixth of one per cent. of sulphur in iron develops red shortness. Now you may take one ton of cold short iron, containing one half of one per cent. of phosphorus and no sulphur, and mix it with one ton of red short iron, containing one sixth of one per cent. of sulphur, and no phosphorus, and both impurities are so diluted in the mass, that they are insufficient to cause the total to exhibit either cold shortness or hot shortness, but unless eliminated in some other way, both of them remain in the iron, now to the extent of phosphorus one quarter of one per cent., and sulphur one twelfth of one per cent. The fact that the result, in cases like the foregoing, gave a comparatively neutral iron, led to the conclusion, which I am aware was extensively held, and still prevails somewhat, that each was neutralized by the other, when really, in my judgment, the effect was only produced by the dilution of both. Indeed, in the partial analysis given, showing an ore containing forty-eight per cent. metallic iron, and .12 of one per cent of phosphorus, or ¼ of one per cent. phosphorous in the pig, I do not believe the quantity of phosphorus *was* sufficient to make the iron cold short, and if it *was* enough, the run out so eliminated it, that it did not need the offices of any equally pernicious friend to make the iron good.

I heartily wish that the association was financially able to enlist the assistance of an expert chemist, to make careful analysis of ores, and resultant irons and slag; of run-out metals, and blooms and bars, and their slags; and any chemical difference in the several grades of pig, or if you chose, in pig that *will*, and that which will *not chill.* By every legitimate means we must elucidate these doubtful matters, just as we must practice every known economy, and study to place ourselves above apprehensions as to unfavorable legislation, by improving the quality of our products, increasing our out-put, avoiding waste, reducing cost, extending the field of use, and conducting all our operations in a spirit of friendly and honorable competition, but as in its continual presence, with the assurance that thus we are being fitted for the severest competition with all processes at home, and for anything with which foreign countries can confront us.

The address of Col. Wiestling being before the Association for discussion, the following remarks were made:

Mr. W. T. Hildrup, of Harrisburg, Pennsylvania. Mr. President, will you allow an "outsider" to give a few facts in reference to the chill of anthracite iron, which chills equally well with charcoal iron. There has been an impression (which I have also had for 30 years or more) that, in making car wheels, hot blast iron cannot, or will not, chill with cold blast iron. I have used Saulsbury cold blast iron that would chill three fourths of an inch, and throw kish in the sprue. I am using a hot blast Saulsbury iron of the highest grade that shows a small paper chill.

The President. Do we understand the gentleman to say that he has anthracite iron that will chill as deep as charcoal iron?

Mr. Hildrup. Yes, sir; I have anthracite iron, which you would term, possibly, No. 2, that will chill three eighths of an inch; No. 2½, or a low classification of No. 3, that will chill half an inch; and a No. 3, that will chill from three quarters to an inch. I can show gentlemen the specimens, and will be pleased to give them all the information they desire, at my office.

You will, perhaps, allow me to say another thing: That charcoal iron, that is rated as the best wheel iron, is very moderate in its transverse strength. You may be astonished, probably, at the announcement of the fact that a bar four feet long, one inch thick, and two inches wide, resting on the ends, and broken by a weight on the center, that the best Saulsbury will carry between 1,600 and 1,700 before it breaks; and that the anthracite iron I spoke of will carry from 2,700 to 3,000 pounds before it breaks. Yet I know no anthracite iron I could trust as car wheel iron.

Col. Wiestling. I will be very much gratified if the gentleman indorses one half of what I say. The impression is among charcoal men that this mysterious property is monopolized by charcoal iron, which I do not believe.

Mr. Milnes, of Shenandoah Iron Works, Virginia. Suppose that both the anthracite and charcoal iron have an equal chilling property, is not the charcoal iron stronger in the wheels? Is it not more ductile? Is there not more tenacity? Or does the gentleman think that there is about the same tenacity in anthracite iron, as now made by the most approved methods?

Mr. Hildrup. The tensile strength we have not tested, but the shrinkage of iron is a question of great importance. It is not the strongest iron that makes the best car wheel. I have tried some hot blast No. 2, that chills five eighths of an inch, which was very good car wheel iron; or, at least, had the evidence of being such. I think the data that we have at our office would interest many of you gentlemen. It is at your service.

Mr. Coffin, of Muirkirk Furnace, Maryland. In regard to tensile strength, I have never seen or heard of anthracite iron that would stand over 25,000 pounds to the square inch. I have seen charcoal iron that would stand 40,000, and even higher than that.

Mr. Hildrup. I can give no facts in reference to that; I have no data.

Mr. Birkinbine, of Philadelphia. I think we have in the chilling property of the iron, the tempering property of steel, and the welding property of iron, what we may call analogous conditions. From the experiments and tests that have been made within the past few years, I incline to the belief that, other things being the same, iron of equal purity chills and welds, and steel of equal purity tempers according to the amount of carbon combined in the metal. I do not say that we can demonstrate this now, but all of our experiments have tended that way. In reference to tenacity we all know that if we had a pig of white iron it might break quite easily if thrown down, and yet stand a greater tensile strain than the gray iron, yet no one avers that white iron is stronger than the gray.

A few months since visiting a large car wheel works, I saw a pile of iron brought from a furnace so far away, and past so many others, that I was anxious to know more about it, as I had not learned that the iron was remarkable for its chilling properties; and yet the proprietor said it was the best he had on his banks. He gave as the reason, "It is always the same." It seems to me that this is a point that every manufacturer of charcoal iron should always have in view. What iron men want to study is, to keep their product ALWAYS THE SAME. Let us stick to the quality, and keep that up, and we need have no fear about our making the purest iron, and that best adapted for car-wheel or other special purposes.

Mr. Hildrup. I can say, and most emphatically, that I do not believe in anthracite iron for car wheels. I simply made the remark I did on chilling quality as a matter of fact.

Col. Wiestling. There is one requisite absolutely indispensable in all our experiments, and that is, the conditions should be the same. In the history of the iron and steel interests of our country, it is perfectly simple for us now to look back and see how iron, especially iron rails, that were made solely of pigs with the run out, and obtained from the most impure stock, was suddenly brought into direct competition with steel rails, made out of charcoal iron and the purest of ores; and it is the case to-day. Your steel at the Bessemer works is made out of ores with the very best indorsements on them, and without any impurity that will tend to make the iron brittle; and if you take that steel as against iron made of impure stocks, of course, it is all on one side. I say it is impossible to have good anthracite iron made out of a good quality of ore, without a good flux. With the ore not inferior and the flux not inferior, the anthracite will be the better. So I said that the conditions should always be the same. Take the same ores and the same limitations of manufacture, and iron out of charcoal, having a purer fuel, will have a purer product than with any other fuel that is impure.

Correction of Minutes.

In transcribing and printing the minutes of the first session of the annual meeting, the following omission occurs:

"The President announced that the Board of Managers recommended as honorary and corresponding members of the Association: I. Lowthian Bell, England; Prof. Richard Akermann, Sweden; Dr. Hermann Wedding, Prussia; A. S. McCreath, Harrisburg, Pa.; Prof. F. B. Hough, Lowville, N. Y.

"The recommendation was adopted by acclamation."

This omission was not discovered until the minutes were in print, and the correction hence occurs in this place.

Notes on the Desulphurization of Ore by the Westman Kiln, at Katahdin Iron Works, Me.

By OWEN W. DAVIS, JR.*

The ore originally worked at the Katahdin Iron Works was a limonite, occurring in beds on the side of a hill, at an elevation of two hundred (200) to three hundred (300) feet above the river.

These beds appear to have been formed by the gradual precipitation of the iron in solution, in the water of mineral springs that have broken out on the hillside, several such springs now existing there, and depositing ore with surprising rapidity.

Average samples of the ore show:

Sesqui-oxide of iron,	73.5	per cent.
Magnesia,	1.2	"
Alumina,	1.3	"
Lime,	1.0	"
Silica,	4.2	"
Sulphur,	1.2	"
Phosphorus,	0.035	"
Water,	16.5	"
Metallic iron,	51.45	"

The sulphur being present mainly as a sulphate.

This ore was roasted in heaps, on piles of wood, and readily yielded most of the combined water, and a large per cent. of the sulphur, and when fairly well roasted in this manner, it produced, with ten per cent. of lime and a hot furnace, a very handsome open-grained iron, very soft and fluid, showing silicon 2 to 3 per cent., sulphur trace to .07 per cent., and phosphorus 0.06 to 0.10 per cent. But the action of the furnace was irregular, and unsatisfactory; changes and slips being frequent and sudden, and all the iron above the grade of the soft No. I X, above referred to, showing a lack of strength, and an unhealthy fracture not to be expected in a good charcoal iron. Occasional analyses of sam-

*** Read at the annual meeting of the U. S. Association of Charcoal Iron Workers at Chambersburg, Pa., October 20, 1880.**

ples of iron sent away for test, showed an excessive and unusual amount of silicon, which varied but slightly in the different grades, from No. 1 to white iron.

About the year 1877 the beds of surface ore began to give out, and it was found that underlying these beds was a formation of pyritiferous rock, very easily decomposed, in which the pyrites occur, not as cubical crystals, but in layers, like mica. This formation has become changed, *insitu*, to a hydrated oxide of iron, the ore occurring irregularly, and without any uniformity, and the rock in many places passing imperceptibly into ore, while in others the ore rests on the surface of the rock, sharply separated. The deposit has been opened in many places within a radius of half a mile, and worked extensively in six different openings, starting in each case on the hillside, where the ground rises rapidly.

In these places the ore is found mixed with the ledge to a depth of ten to twenty feet when the "blue ledge" is ordinarily encountered, which, near the surface, is friable and soft, but at depth of a few inches becomes hard, with a metallic ring.

This kind of ore is abundant, but carries more sulphur than the surface ore, and in the shape of a sulphide, which, at a red heat, cannot be reduced further than to FeS, but for its complete decomposition requires an intense oxidizing heat.

Analysis of this ore shows:

Sesqui-oxide of iron,	68	per cent.
Magnesia,	1	"
Alumina,	4	"
Lime,	1.50	"
Silica,	7.80	"
Sulphur,	3	"
Phosphorus,	.02	"
Water,	15	"
Metallic iron,	47.6	"

The furnace was put at work upon this ore without our fully realizing the increased amount of sulphur present in it, and much trouble ensued. Each day's work showed nearly every grade of iron, from 1 to 6, while working on same burden, and it was found very difficult, with any heat attainable, to keep the furnace upon a grade of soft iron, a half day's run on this grade being certainly followed by sudden changes to white iron.

Every expedient known for lowering—in the blast furnace—the amount of silicon and sulphur in the iron, was carefully tried. Limestone charges, varying from 5 to 50 per cent., were thoroughly tested, and analyses of the resulting irons showed very slight variations in the silicon and sulphur present.

Mixing calcined lime with the ore made no apparent difference. The furnace boshes were then carried up from 60° to 70° pitch, in a stack 36'x9', and more blast added. The result was a large product (some fifteen tons daily) of an exceedingly poor iron—porous, spongy, white, with a dull, unhealthy fracture. Samples of this iron, afterwards analyzed, showed silicon and sulphur excessive, viz:

	No. 4 pig.	No. 5 pig.	No. 6 pig.
Silicon, ...	2.74	2.22	3.89
Sulphur, ...	.30	.62	.66

The iron being graded according to the fracture.

At this time a series of arches made of stone piers, with pigs of iron covering the openings between, were built for roasting the ore. As more uniformity in roasting was thereby obtained, a resulting improvement in the iron was noticed. At this time, in order to give the ore better opportunity for reduction, fifteen feet were added to the height of the stack, with a decided improvement in quality of iron and fuel consumption, but the iron was still unsatisfactory and the silicon obstinately high.

This was the state of affairs in the winter of 1878. It seemed apparent to the writer, at that time, that the outlook for the iron trade was such as to encourage the belief in better times in the ensuing spring, and to warrant some further effort at overcoming the difficulty; and it was then determined to make a thorough investigation into the causes of our trouble, in the hope of removing them.

To accomplish this, a chemical laboratory was fitted up at the works, and we were fortunate in securing the services of Mr. Ernst Sjöstedt, of Sweden, a graduate of the school of mines at Stockholm, to conduct the investigation.

Complete analyses of ores, iron, fluxes, and cinders from recent and former blasts were made, and it very soon became evident that our real antagonist had been, not silicon, but sulphur, which met us on every hand and in quantities much greater than anticipated. One analysis after another confirmed the theory that the relation between sulphur and silicon in our pig iron was very intimate, as we found that in every case where the sulphur in the iron was high, 0.20 to 0.60 per cent., the silicon was excessive, 2 to 4 per cent., and this, no matter what the grade of the iron might be, a white hard iron containing 0.60 per cent of sulphur, showing 3 to 4 per cent. silicon, or as high as a soft No. IX that had but a trace of sulphur.

The following analyses of iron, made at previous times, elucidate this point:

Grade.	IX.	1.	2.	3.	4.	5.	6.
Silicon, . . .	4.55	3.09	2.12–2.47	1.86–3.55	1.96–2.74	1.30–2.00	1.07–3.87
Sulphur, . . .	0.01	0.08	0 06–0.30	0.10–0.39	0.20–0.30	0.18–0.62	0.28–0.66

It seemed that the heat necessary to induce the large amount of sulphur to combine with the lime as sulphide of lime, and pass off in the slag, was sufficient to reduce the silicon, which then united with the iron, and forced the carbon (which, in a siliceous iron, would naturally assume a graphitic form,) to appear as combined carbon, in short, that much of our hard mottled iron which showed 2 to 3 per cent. silicon and 0.20 to 0.60 sulphur, with carbon mostly combined, would, but for sulphur, have been soft No. 1 iron, with graphitic carbon.

Analyses of ore (taken from the arches above described) showed that that portion of the ore that had been directly over the wood, and reached a high degree of heat, had parted with its sulphur absolutely, while samples taken midway up to the top of the piles showed relatively increasing amounts, proving that the portion of sulphur existing as sulphate, had disappeared at a moderate heat, while the other compound, the sulphide, was affected only by an intense oxydising heat. How then to arrange it that every portion of the ore could be raised to that degree of heat necessary to break up this compound, and to do it uniformly, regularly, and on a large scale, was the problem presented to us. It was believed that this could be accomplished by a calcining kiln of the general design and arrangement of the Westman kiln, so common in Sweden, and a kiln of this character was devised by Mr. Sjöstedt, assisted by our agent, Mr. George D. Colby, but designed for using wood instead of gas, as is generally the case in Sweden. This kiln is a cylindrical shaft 22′ in height to the filling doors, expanding in diameter from 4′ 8″ at top, to 10′ at bottom; built of red brick, and lined with fire-brick to height of 10′, and the whole bound together with five iron bands 4′ wide. The base is perforated with six radial passages for drawing the ore, increasing in width from 2′ 6″ at outer circumference, to 5′ 2″ on inner circumference; the walls of kiln at bottom being 3′ thick, and tapering to 1′ at top. The tops of these drawing arches are covered with heavy iron plates, above these are double the number or twelve fire arches, 20″ wide, for receiving the wood, and opening directly into the kiln. The walls at the fire arches are 2′ 9″ thick, and the structure here is twelve sided, each face being covered with heavy iron plates hooked at the joints with wrought iron rods to allow for expansion, and the door and ash-hole being cast in the plates. Two feet above the arches are six small openings for inserting bars whenever the stock gets clinkered above the fire arches. As thus built the kiln was fired, but the ore being very friable, the draft was not sufficient, and a chimney was added with 4′ flue, 35′ in height. The first results were encouraging, the roasted ore showing but .05 to .15 per cent. sulphur, and the iron made from this ore exhibiting excellent fracture with silicon down to 1 per cent. But even with the high chimney, it was soon found that the sulphur sublimed and settled back upon the ore the longer the kiln was worked, the draft being still insufficient, and the old and too familiar silicon ran up again to 3 and 4 per cent. in the iron. Samples taken at this time, showed:

Grade.	No. 2.	No. 4.	No. 4.	3.	6.
Silicon, ...	3.76	3.75	3.31	3.59	1.51
Sulphur, ...	.13	.08	.17	.13	.09

And the kiln up to this point was a failure. But enough had been seen of the practical working of it to warrant a belief in its complete success, if some way could be devised for carrying off the sulphur after once separated from the ore.

A wrought-iron pipe 16″ in diameter, and 12′ long, was lowered into the kiln at the center, the top of the pipe projecting about two feet above the filling doors into the chimney, and it was at once apparent that we were on the right track, the draft being much improved, and the amount of ore passing through the kiln more than doubling, the sulphur passing freely up through the bottom of the pipe. With this arrangement at work, the roasting was more uniform; the sulphur in ore decreased from 2 and 3 per cent. to .02 to .10 per cent., and under precisely similar conditions in the blast furnace as before; the silicon decreased very materially, as shown by the following:

Grade.	No. 3.	4.	4½.	5.	6.
Silicon,	1.04	.72	.67	.62	.57
Sulphur,	.05	.03	.05	.03	.06

This pipe, being a temporary expedient, was removed, and a fire brick pier was built in the center of the kiln, with an inside diameter of 17″, to height of 12′, with walls tapering from 19″ to 14″ thick, at distance of 3′. Cast-iron plates, cast with hole 17″ in diameter, were set into the brick work, square openings, 4″×4″, being left on two sides in the outer circumference. Two railroad bars, 24′ long, were fastened into the foundation of kiln, and passed through the openings in plates above described, and secured at top, to hold the pier firmly in place. On top of the brick work rests a heavy ring, cast with a flange, into which sets a wrought-iron flue pipe, 16″ in diameter, that extends upward to a height of two feet above the charging doors, projecting into the chimney. In the circumference of this central pier were left three rows of flues, containing six in each row, and of size 4″×6″, sloping downward, so as to prevent the ore from getting into it, and, at the bottom, a clearing out door was left, covered by an arch to the outer circumference, through which a bar can be inserted for removing dirt that would accumulate, and stop the draft.

This arrangement is now in use at our works, and with results entirely satisfactory. The ore is hauled to doors on a trestling, and dumped, and is there sorted, and broken into lumps, not over 8″×8″, and shoveled into the two doors at top. As the ore descends, it gradually parts with its water, and becomes hotter and, just in front of the fire arches, it reaches a white heat just on the point of fusion, when the sulphur is freed, and passes up into the flues of the pier, and rolls out in great volumes at top of the chimney.

Passing by the fire, the ore drops below and is drawn out of the drawing doors, while still hot, and falls into troughs containing water, which removes any of sulphur still left in it. As the ore is very much crumbled, it is generally charged into the furnace while still wet, to hinder it from running down through the coal.

The ore from the kiln shows sulphur low, and uniformly so—.03 to .10 per cent., and the working of the furnace is regular.

Our ordinary charge is:

Coal.	Limestone.	Manganese.	Ore.
24 bu.	130 lbs.	10 lbs.	1,200 lbs.

With temperature 600°, and pressure $1\frac{3}{4}$ to 2 pounds, and we run through 50 to 60 charges daily, with a product of 14 to 16 tons wheel iron.

Analysis of cinder from above charge gives:

$Si. O_2$, ...	50.450 per cent.,	containing O,	26.9
$Fe. O_3$, ...	7.32		
Al_2, O_3, ...	6.571	containing O,	3.06
Mn. O, ...	1.65		.34
Ca. O, ...	26.30		7.51
Mg. O, ...	7.62		3.05

Showing nearly a bi-silicate to which we aim to keep.

With such a charge, the resulting pig iron is of a superior quality, of great strength, and shows a high chill, and is selling freely for car wheels to some of the largest car wheel shops in the country.

As compared with other well known brands of iron, it takes high rank in actual use, and as shown by the following comparative analyses of samples, most of them taken from different wheel foundries by the writer, and analyzed by Mr. Sjöstedt or Mr. Colby:

	Stickney, 4½.	Copake, No. 3.	Detroit, No. 3.	Millerton.	Salisbury.	Katahdin.
Combined carbon,	0.75	0.74	0.48	0.68	0.72	0.60
Graphitic carbon,	1.84	2.63	2.49	3.07	2.22	2.84
Silicon, ...	.65	1.24	.61	1.01	1.58	.75
Sulphur, ...	.04	.04	.035	.03	.03	.049
Phosphorus, . .	.19	.21	.08	.19	.31	.07
Manganese, . . .	.66	—	—	—	.37	.10

For the past two months our kiln has roasted an average of 38.75 tons of ore daily, at a cost of 47.70 cents per ton, as follows:

	Daily.
Horse and cart, ½ day, ...	$1 25
Tools, ...	50
1 man, ...	1 55
2 men, $1 45, ...	2 90
6 men, $1 30, ...	7 80
3 cords wood, $1 50, ...	4 50
	$18 50

Or, 47.7 per ton.

With ore thus roasted, we find little difficulty in keeping the furnace in good condition, and with excellent results, as our product for past six weeks has averaged 108.19 tons per week, of Nos. 3, 4, 4½, and 5 iron, with average fuel consumption of 94.88 bushels (of 2,688 cubic inches) to the ton of iron on an ore yielding 47.35 per cent. iron, and for the past week we made 104¼ tons, with a consumption of 88.4 bushels of coal on a 48.3 per cent. ore, or about one ton of iron to two cords of wood.

DISCUSSION.

The President having announced the subject open for discussion,

Mr. Birkinbine said: Mr. President, the paper that Mr. Davis has read is one of interest, not only to all charcoal iron workers, but equally of interest to the users of anthracite and coke. Mr. Davis seems determined to save his fuel by lessening the work in his furnace; and we all know this is the best way. There is no better economy than a thorough preparation of the material in the stock-house, and the selection of proper ores. We have present a number of gentlemen well qualified to speak on this important subject. Mr. Meily has roasted ores largely in heaps and kilns. Mr. Sjöstedt, from Sweden, is conversant with the Westman kilns, and I have a paper here describing them in connection with a Swedish iron works, and drawings illustrating their construction. We also have here a gentlemen who has tried more methods of desulphurizing, and more shapes and sizes of kilns, probably, than any of us. I refer to Mr. Jones Wister, of Harrisburg. [Applause.] I move that Mr. Wister be invited to address the Association upon the subject.

The motion was carried by acclamation.

Mr. Wister. I must thank you for this very kind invitation, but the gentleman who preceded me, (Mr. Davis,) has said so much, and to the point, about the desulphurization of iron ores; he has gone into such minute detail, and covered the ground so thoroughly, and his conclusions are so much like my own, that anything I should say would be simply corroborative of what he has said. We are all aiming to get rid of this terrible enemy, sulphur. I may say that we worked nearly ten years on highly sulphurous ores, without the success which we were aiming for. It has been only the past two or three years that we have found out what an enemy sulphur is. Since then we have been working ores originally containing little sulphur. With ores of this character we are producing far better results than we ever did from roasted ores. Our kilns were not first-rate ones; they were experimental. With them we obtained varying results, which were not what we wanted; and we have, therefore, in a very great measure, given up roasting ores. We have been using large amounts of foreign ores, because they carry little or no sulphur. With these ores we are now operating, and find our success much greater than with ores containing sulphur, which we imperfectly desulphurized. I will simply add that anything Mr. Davis has said, I will corroborate. We have not gone so much into detail as he, but our conclusions are the same as those he has reached. When we do not have any sulphur, we have the best results.

President Wiestling. What was the fuel used?

Mr. Wister. Anthracite coal, about pea size, produced better results than large coal.

President Wiestling. Was the general shape of the kiln such as described by Mr. Davis?

Mr. Wister. No; not at all. We used two styles of kilns. The first one was 45 feet high, constructed and patented by Charles Atkins, for roasting Cornwall ores. He first roasted Cornwall ore in these kilns. There were three combustion chambers below for the fuel. The gas issuing from these chambers was supposed to draw up through the ore, and roast it; but it did not. We abandoned the plan, and used fuel in direct contact with the ore more successfully; but none of these kilns have thoroughly deprived Cornwall ore of its sulphur. Our kilns now in use are about fifteen feet high, and are the best kilns we have used for roasting Cornwall ores. Those now generally used are 17 feet in diameter, about 15 feet high, built with a bosh, (somewhat like a blast furnace,) with holes through the lower portion, through which bars can be thrust to break up the ore, as it melts fast. Those who use these kilns get excellent results. But we have given up the use of kilns, and use ores that have little sulphur in them.

Mr. Davis. I have a kiln that may be objectionable, as we fire with wood. The Westman kiln, in Sweden, is run with waste gases from blast furnaces. We desire to operate a kiln, in a good many instances, when the furnace is not in blast. I have no idea that the kiln I have described would supply our furnaces. I expect to build several. But I find it does what is done comparatively cheap. I have found it much better to make a kiln for wood than one for gas; and it, perhaps, serves our purposes better than it would those in Pennsylvania.

Mr. Willard Warner. Would it be practicable to use charcoal?

Mr. Davis. I think it would. All you want to get is heat to the center of the kiln. It is, of course, desirable to have more or less flame, and well that you have gas sufficient. We have found that essential to the operation and continuing in use of the Westman kiln. I do not think the gentleman will have any difficulty.

Mr. J. Meily, of Lebanon, Pennsylvania. Speaking in reference to the kilns described by Mr. Wister, I would say that he got the draft of it from the "Jgers furnace," or roaster. It is a Swedish furnace, and gives, with us, very good results. The first was built for Mr. Dawson Coleman, which is standing to-day, at North Lebanon, and used with very fair success. The one at our furnace is somewhat modified, but gives generally satisfactory results. There is, also, one in use at the furnaces along the Reading railroad, near the Schuylkill river. I am now sending charcoal dust from the forge to the furnace, and the ore is being roasted with very excellent results.

Mr. Warner. Would the process described answer well for the simple work of calcining ores, without reference to sulphur?

Mr. Meily. I think this process is cheaper than any I know of. The kiln is 16 feet at boshes; the height same as described. It sets up from the ground about 2 feet. Forming the center of the kiln is a truncated cone, upon which there rests another cone that flanges out beyond the lower one. The air for combustion comes from the outside, through an underground drain, and then is sent up into the cone, and enters the center of the mass of ore. We can roast, with two furnaces, 200 or 300 hundred tons of ore per week, depending upon the ore itself, and the quality of it roasted, as we have what are known as the "lean" and "select" ores. But the members of the Association will understand the ores better than I can tell, when we reach Cornwall. The term does not mean selected ore, but the run of the best. The fine, soft Cornwall ore is somewhat like a powder, which, when subjected to heat, acts like quicksand, or has the peculiarity of running, and the sulphur is so intimately wrought into the ore that the smallest particles of it will carry sulphur to a great extent. The great difficulty has been that the fine ore would clog up the draft and put the fires out. It is so dense, and packs so intimately, and the particles join together so firmly, that the draft naturally will not penetrate through it. Therefore, the idea of this kiln is, that this motion of the body of ore, resting on the sharp, pointed cone, the cone acts as a great wedge, to stop it from packing, to break the mass, and allow the draft to pass up.

But I think I am drifting away from the gentleman's question. He asked me if it would be a cheap mode of roasting ores just for calcination. I reply it would be cheaper than any process I know of, unless immense heaps were roasted and washed afterwards.

I would just add that we are roasting this ore at considerably less than 25 cents per ton to-day; but not having any data conveniently at hand, I cannot give the exact amount. One ton of pea coal is what we used to use for 40 tons of ore, but with charcoal dust, we take more of the braize, that is, our own braize. The lowest cost for roasting I would fix is at 18 cents. In all pit charcoal dust there is apt to be little stones, carrying silica, and that would add to the amount of silica in the ore. There is also much debris that does not burn. I fill from the railroad trestle directly from cars. If the roaster be full in the evenings, and where there are two of these roasters, they will supply the blast furnace over night by lowering the roaster two or three fillings. They are filled up again in the morning—a layer of coal spread over, say an 1 in depth, and then a layer of ore, say 18 inches in depth.

Mr. Lobdell, Delaware. Any draft stack?

Mr. Miley. No draft stack at all, the smoke sailing off all the time.

Mr. Lobdell. What is the cost?

Mr. Miley. I will undertake to contract for one for about $500. They can be seen right in Lebanon.

Mr. Warner. When we fill with from one to three thousand pounds of coal, with a heavy layer of ore over that, the draft drags. It is not a very satisfactory method, and we would be glad to find a better way.

Mr. Miley. The point claimed for the Jgers kiln is the almost absolute uniformity obtained in the results. Whether it has reached the greatest degree of perfection remains to be seen.

Mr. Warner. The great trouble is the roasting of large lumps.

Mr. Miley. They ought to be broken up.

President Wiestling. The paper of Mr. Davis, and the discussion properly refer to the use of kilns for desulphurizing processes, but the remarks of our Vice President bring out the idea of applying the methods that are used at Lebanon for other ores.

The different ores of this valley* are mostly hematites, having very little sulphur in them. They contain hygroscopic water to the extent of 10 or 12 per cent., and considerable combined water. My impression is, that in the highly sulphurous ores, you can roast them with a very small amount of fuel, because you have the benefit of the sulphur in roasting. I do not suppose with any kind of kilns there would be difficulty with the brown hematite in lumps, but the difficulty is when you wash your ores, for then it chokes the draft. With any experiments that we have made, we have found that difficulty. We could burn 15 or 20 tons a day of lumps, but only get 3 or 4 tons a day of fine ore. As I understand, Mr. Ernst Sjöstedt is here and represents the Westman kiln. We would be very happy to hear from him.

Mr. E. Sjöstedt. Not having sufficient command of the English language, I would really be consuming the valuable time of the Association in your attempting to listen to me. But all the information I can I will gladly give the members of the Association.

Mr. Birkinbine. Will the gentleman favor us with them in a paper at some future time?

Mr. Sjöstedt. Yes, sir; I will try and have a prepared paper at the next meeting of Association.

The President. Since the discussion of this matter of the Swedish kiln and the Westman kiln has been brought forward this evening, we will be glad to hear directly from the far off land of Sweden. We are honored this evening with the presence of Hon. Le Comte C. Lewenhaupt, Swedish counsel to the United States, and I know we would all be glad to hear from him. (Applause.)

Hon. Le Comte C. Lewenhaupt. I only beg leave to thank you gentleman for inviting me to this meeting, and to state that this invitation will be considered as a friendly greeting from our American brethern to the manufacturers of charcoal iron of my country, who have the honor to be known to gentlemen present. I beg you will excuse me from talking further, but you will allow me to keep my ears open and my mouth shut. (Laughter and applause.)

*Cumberland valley.

The Manufacture of Charcoal in Kilns.

Extracts from a Paper Read before the American Institute of Mining Engineers.

BY T. EGLESTON, PH.D., NEW YORK CITY.

The manufacture of charcoal in kilns was declared many years ago, after a series of experiments, made in poorly constructed furnaces, to be unprofitable, and the subject is dismissed by most writers with the remark that in order to use the method economically the products of distillation, both liquid and gaseous, must be collected. Some authors speak in a doubtful way of the quality of the charcoal produced, and a few concede that, with great care, good charcoal can be made in kilns, but that most of the workmen do not like kiln charcoal. This is the real secret of the opposition to this method of manufacture.

Until recently, therefore, the manufacturers of charcoal iron have considered meiler or pit coal superior to kiln-made coal, but the manufacture of this latter kind of coal has been so much improved of late years that it is sometimes difficult for the advocates of meiler coal to distinguish the difference between the two.

The question of pit or kiln coal was formerly settled by the cost of transportation. When transportation was low, kilns were used, the advantage of output being greatly in their favor, since the kiln can be burned slow or fast, to make the coal of requisite density. The yield of charcoal is also greater in the kiln than in the meiler, it being from 45 to 50 bushels to the cord in the kiln, and from 30 to 35 in the meiler. The amount of labor in using the kiln is also less. To counterbalance the increase in yield, the decrease in labor, the security against accident, and the celerity of the operation, the cost of transportation will have to be high. Besides this, the kiln is always under complete control, and can be examined by the burner at any time, and the exact condition of every part of it can be ascertained at every step in the process. As there is only an approximate knowledge and control of the meiler, the kiln should give the best product. The possibility of a large output is, however, the *ignis fatuus* of modern metallurgy. The kilns are "turned" so often that the charcoal is burned too rapidly, and the quality becomes poor. Experience has shown that it is more economical to use kilns of small capacity, and that the increase in the cost of the structures is more than compensated for by the increase in the quality of the product; while with large kilns the diminished cost of the plant is dearly purchased at the expense of a diminished yield of coal, and by the relatively poor quality of the product. The charcoal manufactured in kilns is cleaner, since it is free from the sand of the cover of the meiler, and is also denser if the process is conducted slowly. The yield is at least from 15 to 20 per cent. more, and the expense is at least one third less. In addition to this, as the meilers are at a distance, there is a loss of charcoal in transportation, amounting to 10 to 15 per cent., so that the total gain in kiln manufacture is from 25 to 30 per cent. If the process was conducted as slowly, there is little donbt that the kiln coal would be equal, if not superior to the meiler coal.

Kilns for the manufacture of charcoal are made of almost any shape and size, determined, in most cases, by the fancy of the builder, or by the necessities of the shape of the ground selected. They do not differ from each other in any principle of manufacture, nor does there seem to be any appreciable difference in the quality of the fuel they produce, when the process is conducted with equal care in the different varieties; but there is a considerable difference in the yield and in the cost of the process in favor of small over large kilns. The different varieties have come into and gone out of use mainly on account of the cost of construction and of repairs. The object of a kiln is to replace the cover of a meiler by a permanent structure.

The kilns which are used may be divided into the *rectangular*, the *round*, and the *conical*, but the first two seem to be disappearing before the last, which is as readily built and much more easily managed. All varieties of kilns are usually built of red brick, or, rarely, of brick and stone together. Occasionally refractory brick is used, but it is not necessary. The foundations are usually made of stone. The brick should be sufficiently hard to resist the fire, and should, therefore, be tested before using. As the pyroligneous acid which results from the distillation of the wood, attacks lime mortar, it is best to lay up the brick with fire-clay mortar, to which a little salt has been added; sometimes loam mixed with coal-tar, to which a little salt is also added, is used. Special care must be taken in laying the bricks, that every joint is broken, and frequent headers put in to tie the bricks together. All the joints should be carefully filled, as any small open spaces would admit air, and would materially decrease the yield of the kiln. The floor of the kiln was formerly made of two rows of brick set edgewise and carefully laid, but latterly it is found to be best made of clay. Any material, however, that will pack hard may be used. The center must be about 6 inches higher than the sides, which are brought up to the bottom of the lower vents. Most kilns are carefully pointed, and are then painted on the outside with a wash of clay suspended in water, and covered with a coating of coal-tar, which makes them waterproof, and does not require to be renewed for several years.

The largest yield got from kilns is from 50 to 60 bushels for hard wood to 50 for soft wood. The kiln charcoal is very large, so that the loss in fine coal is much diminished. The pieces usually come out the whole size, and sometimes the whole length, of the wood.

DIMENSIONS OF RECTANGULAR KILNS.

	1.	2.	3.	4.
Length,	50	40	40	48
Width,	12	15	14	17
Height,	12	15	18	18
Capacity in cords,	55	70	75	90

1 and 2. Used in New England. 3. Type of those used in Mexico. 4. Kiln at Lauton, Michigan.

A kiln of the size of No. 4, as constructed at the Michigan

Central Iron works, with a good burn, will yield 4,000 bushels of charcoal.

The vertical walls, in the best constructions, are 12 to 13 feet high and 1½ brick thick, containing from 20 to 22 brick to the cubic foot of wall. They are sometimes provided with buttresses, as at Wassaic, N. Y., Fig. 3; but many of them are built without them, as at Lauton, Mich., Figs. 1 and 2. In both cases, they are supported with strong braces, made of round or hewn wood, or of cast iron, which are buried in the ground below, and are tied above and below with iron rods, as in Figs. 1, 2, and 3, the lower end passing beneath the floor of the kiln. They are sometimes tied at the top with wooden braces of the same size, which are securely fastened by iron rods running through the corners, as in Figs. 1 and 2. When a number of kilns are built together, Fig. 2, only the end kilns are braced in this way. The intermediate ones are supported below by wooden braces, securely fastened at the bottom.

Fig. 1.

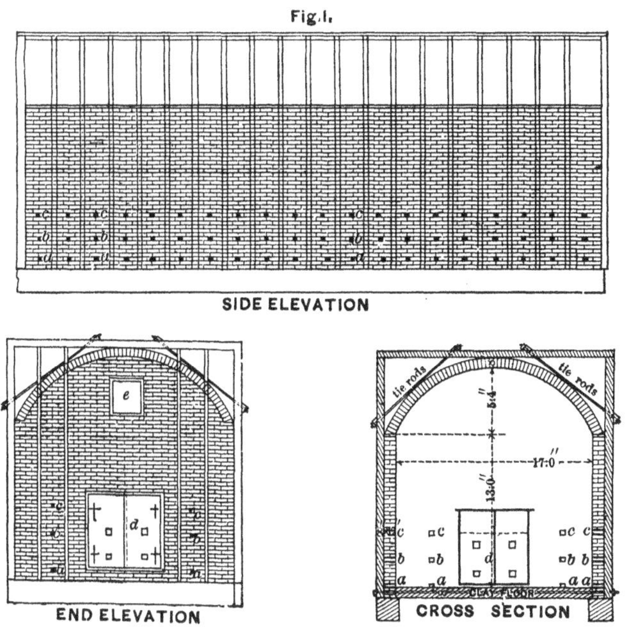

It requires from 35 M. to 40 M. brick for a kiln of 45 cords, and 60 M. to 65 M. for one of 90 cords.

The doors are made of cast iron, in two parts, or of a single piece of sheet iron. On the sides, between the braces or but-

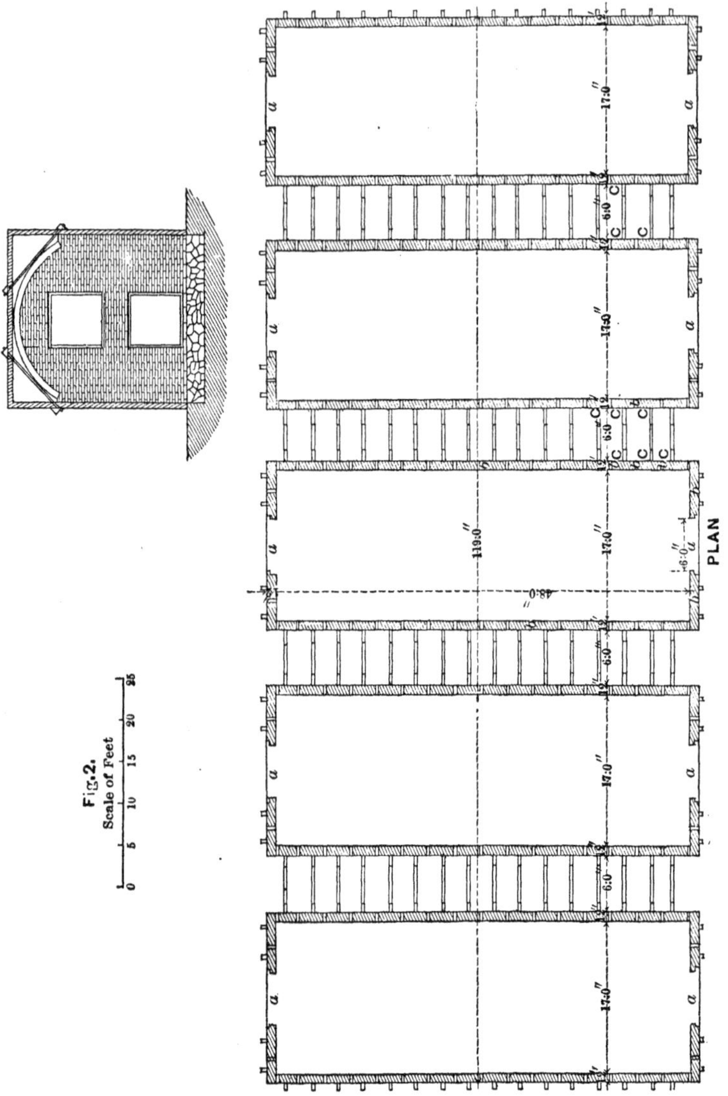

tresses, there are rows of openings, called vent-holes, regularly spaced, vertically and horizontally, for the introduction of the air necessary for combustion, and to allow the products of distillation to escape. Vertically, there are three or four of these, three being the most common number in this part of the country.

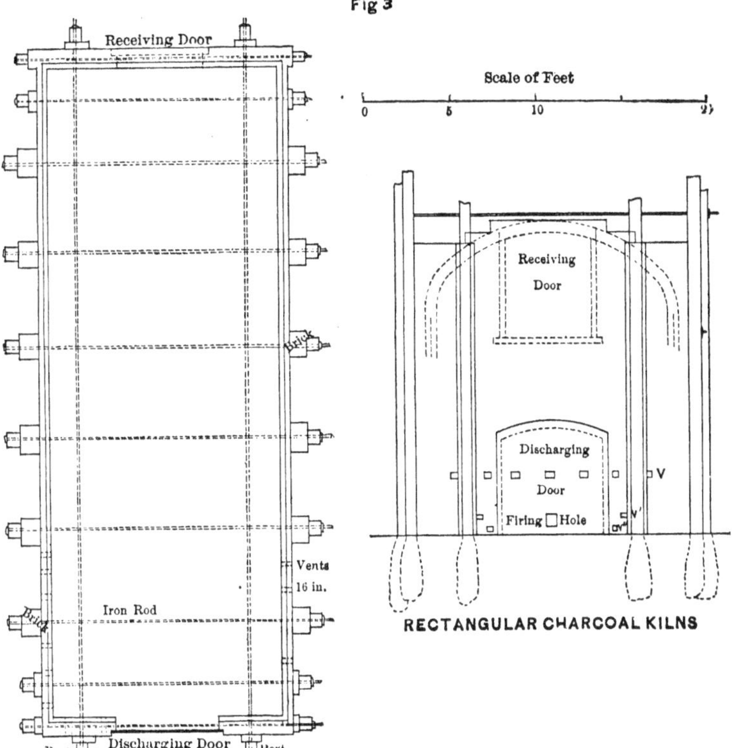

RECTANGULAR CHARCOAL KILNS

The lower one, Fig. 1, is called the foot vent, the middle one the knee vent, and the upper one the shoulder vent. These openings are usually of a size to admit a single brick. They are placed on the level of the ground and up to a height of 1 and 2 feet.

The wood is usually laid flat, piled as closely as possible, so as to leave very few interstices. Stronger charcoal would probably be produced if it were placed on end, but the extra cost of labor to pile it in this way would more than compensate in expense for the extra quality. Four men, working one day, are required to fill a 45-cord kiln. When the fire is kindled, the doors and the opening in the roof are carefully luted with lime mortar. If the clay used in coating the walls was used, it would crack and admit air. Lime mortar must also be used in closing the vents, after the charge is ready to be extinguished.

In Sweden, where these kilns were first used, they were always fired from a permanent structure in the center of the kiln, to which access could be had from the outside. When first used in New England, they were lighted in one corner. The fire was then drawn along the long side, and so round the kiln on the outside of the wood, so that the heat acted directly on the walls. Such a direct exposure rapidly destroyed the mortar in the walls, which became cracked, and the yield of the wood in charcoal was materially diminished. This method of firing was tedious and uncertain. It required from 20 to 28 days to turn a 65-cord kiln. Twelve to fourteen turns were the most that could be expected of a kiln in a year. The lighting is sometimes done by a chimney left in the wood in the center of the kiln, from above, exactly as in the meiler, the fire being drawn down by the openings in the sides; this chimney may or may not connect with a channel leading to the discharging door. This method is used in the south and southwest of the United States, and is practiced in Mexico, and is preferred when the kilns are very wide. It is considered by many to give the best results, both as to yield and quality of charcoal.

Sometimes the lighting is done by means of a channel built through the middle of the kiln, having an opening at each door. This is also filled with dry wood and shavings, which are lit from the back door. The fire is then drawn through the wood to the front door by properly manipulating the vents; both doors are closed, as the whole kiln is then lighted. This method is called the *center burn*. In both these last methods, as the fire is generated in the wood, the heat does not affect the walls of the kiln. The time required for these methods is not more than half that of the first method. A 65-cord kiln can be easily turned twice in 4 weeks, which is ample time. As 24 turns can be made in a year, the capacity of the kiln is doubled.

In the Mexican type of furnace (No. 3, p. 6), where the lighting is done from the center, the work is much more slowly done. It takes them 4 days to burn, 6 to cool, and 4 to empty, or 20 days in all, so that only 18 turns a year are made.

If the kiln is opened too soon, water must be pumped in, as the charcoal would take fire. A small quantity is sufficient to extinguish a kiln, as the water above puts out the fire in contact with it, and what soaks through generates steam below, which extinguishes the fire in the interior. When a very dense coal is required, the kiln is allowed to die out, as it is generally thought that cooling with water impairs the value of the charcoal for blast-furnace use.

The whole art of the process consists in closing the vent-holes at the proper time. One man by day and one by night can easily superintend 5 or 6 kilns. He has little to do except to draw the fire regularly down, to watch the color of the smoke so as to close the vents at the proper time, and to fill any cracks that may form. It is always safer to allow the kiln to remain a longer than a shorter time to cool. If the kiln is properly extinguished, 4 men can easily empty it in 1 day. On the floor there will usually be found some badly burned wood; these brands are either put back in the next charge or used for special purposes about the works.

When a large quantity of cnarcoal is required it is generally best to construct the kilns together, as shown in Fig. 2, and in order to facilitate discharging to have a lower door at each end.

STATISTICS OF RECTANGULAR FURNACES.

	New England.	*Mexico.*
Length,	40 feet.	40
Width,	17 "	14
Heighth,	23 "	18
Capacity in cords,	90	75
Yield in bushels to the cord,	50	50
Days for filling,	3	4
Days for burning,	6	6
Days for cooling and discharging,	6	8
Number of thousand brick,	60	50
Size of vent-holes,	$2\frac{1}{2}\times4$ inches.	

	Wassaic.	*Barnum & Richardson.*
Capacity in cords,	70	90
Length in feet,	40	48
Height "	17	18
Width "	14	17
Size of discharging door,	7×7 feet.	5×5 feet.
Size of charging door,	5×7 feet.	28×30 inches.

Number of thousand brick, ...	30	36
Number of cubic feet of wood, ...	312	333
Weight of iron braces, ...	450 lbs.	1200 lbs.
Square feet of sheet iron for doors, . . .	60	90

TIME OF BURNING.

	Side burn.	*Top burn.*	*Centre burn.*
Days of filling, ...	4	4	4
Days of burning, ...	14	6	5
Days of cooling, ...	6	6	3
Days of discharging, ...	4	4	2
Total, ...	28	20	14
Number of turns a year, . .	13	18	24

(*To be continued.*)

THE EDGAR THOMSON STEEL COMPANY, of Pittsburgh, have purchased from Moses Thompson the privilege to mine and remove all iron ore upon three hundred acres of his land, for the sum of $96,000, all risks of quantity and quality being taken by the steel company. Mr. Thompson also sold to the Company the option to take all the ore from an additional three hundred acres for the sum of $100,000, the option to expire next July. The lands are situated in Patton township, Centre county, and the ores are hematite of good quality, being almost entirely free from phosphorus. The Pennsylvania furnace has also been leased by the Edgar Thomson Steel Company. It will be run with coke, instead of charcoal.

IN ROCKLAND TOWNSHIP, Berks county, Pa., there is a chestnut tree which measures in circumference, around the base of the trunk, thirty-eight feet. The lowest limb, fifteen feet from the ground, measures fourteen feet in circumference. It is believed that the tree will yield seventeen cords of wood. It is still in bearing condition.

TECUMSEH FURNACE, Alabama, has now been in continuous blast for five and a half years, and has made on one hearth about 27,500 tons, with the furnace still doing well. We know of no longer campaign for a charcoal furnace than this one of General Warner's.

Fig. 1.

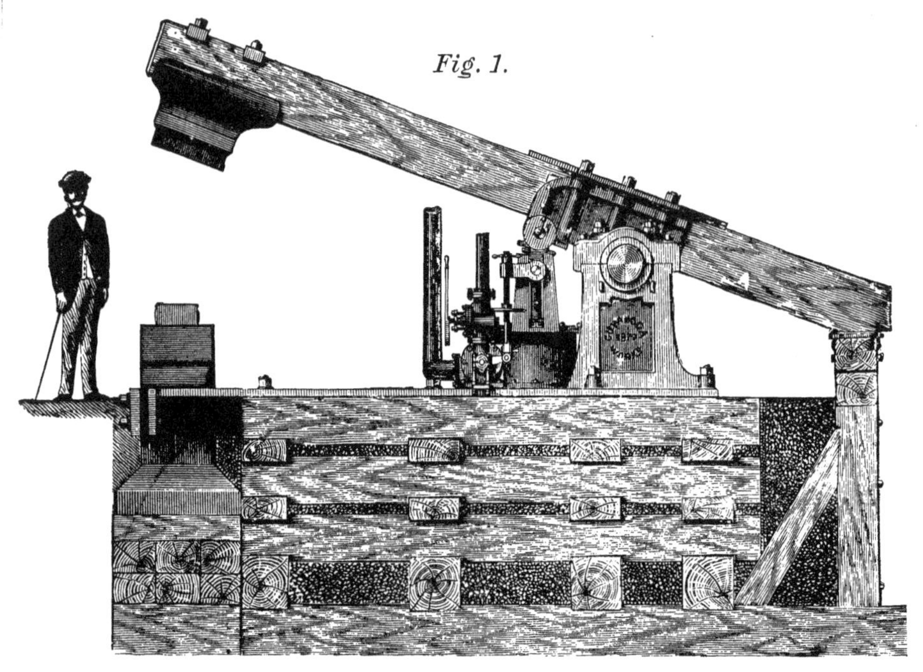

Fig. 2.

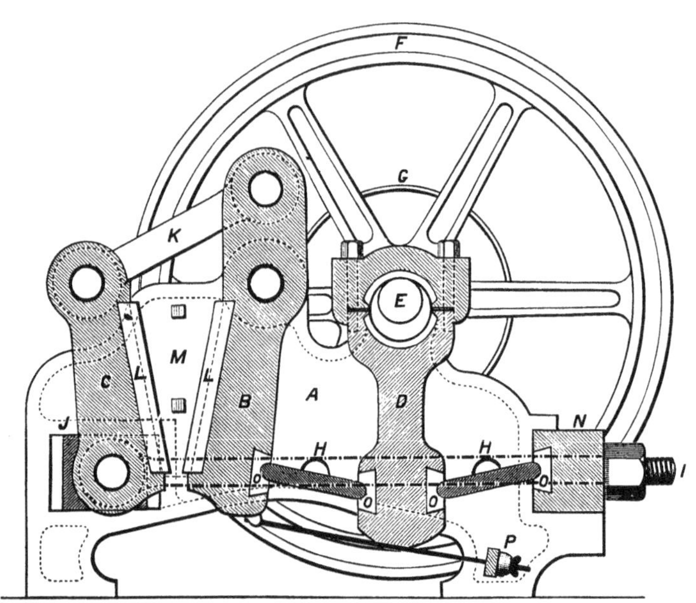

Our Illustrations.

In accordance with our custom of presenting in each number some apparatus or machine of interest to our readers which appears to possess merit, we illustrate in this number Holloway's Steam Helve Hammer, (Fig. 1,) and Buchanan's Rock Breaker, (Fig. 2.)

The former is a forge hammer, consisting of the ordinary wooden helve and iron bits, with husk working in journals. But in place of the cams used in many cases to raise the hammer, motion is given to the helve by a short-stroke vertical steam cylinder, placed in front of the journal bearings.

The helve hammer has been almost inseparably connected with forge work, and many of our bloomery and forge managers will, therefore, be interested in this steam helve hammer, which is manufactured by the Cuyahoga Works, of Cleveland, Ohio.

The peculiarities of construction include a steam-balanced semi-rotating slide valve located on the side of the steam cylinder towards the anvil block, and at the bottom of the cylinder, so as to drain the condensed steam from it. The valve works upon a long, narrow steam port, giving quick action, and a large direct exhaust port permits the hammer to fall freely. They are made of four sizes—1,800, 2,000, 3,000, and 4,000 pounds.

BUCHANAN'S ROCK BREAKER is manufactured at the Union Iron Works, Rockaway, New Jersey, and is claimed to combine lightness with ample strength, and to be a durable machine, economical in the use of applied power, and capable of crushing material rapidly and with uniformity. To permit of transportation, the machine can be separated so that no one piece exceeds 2,000 pounds in weight. By pivoting one jaw at the top and the other at the bottom, a more uniform product, with economy of power, is claimed. The following letters of reference will explain the machine: *A*, main frame; *B*, main jaw; *C*, small jaw; *D*, pitman; *E*, eccentric shaft; *F*, fly wheels; *G*, pulley; *H H*, toggles; *I*, steel tension rod; *J*, adjusting bores; *K*, steel jaw links; *L L*, steel or chilled jaw plates; *M*, chilled side plates; *N*, toggle block; *O O*, toggle bearings; *P*, jaw spring and rod.

A new Charcoal Furnace.

Messrs. Davenport, Fairbairn & Co., of Erie, manufacturers of car-wheels, are constructing a blast furnace at Point St. Ignace, in the northern peninsular of Michigan, just at the straits of Mackinac.

The furnace has been christened "Martel," and will be 53 feet high, and 10½ feet bosh, iron jacket. It will be supplied with two Whitwell stoves, 15 feet in diameter and 60 feet high. The casting-house is a brick structure with iron roof, 43x70 feet; the boiler-house also of brick, 25x36 feet, will contain four boilers 32 feet long and 4 feet in diameter. The engine-house in which will be placed a blowing engine 72 inches in diameter and 4 feet stroke, will be 26½x29½ feet. The stock-house will be 80x170 feet, into which a railway track can be run at a sufficient elevation for unloading ore and fuel direct from the cars. It will be supplied with a steam hoist. The draught stack or chimney will be 162 feet high, with an inside opening of 5 feet.

The owners have a tract of ten acres fronting on the bay, and have constructed a dock into the water sufficiently deep to accommodate the largest vessels. On the tract is a ledge of limestone which is being utilized for building purposes, and which, it is believed, will furnish a cheap and excellent flux. The fuel will be obtained from 15,000 acres of heavy woodland owned by the company, about half of which is situated along the line of the new railway from ten to twelve miles distant, and the other half near the lake shore, from whence the wood or coal can be transported in barges to the furnace dock, at slight cost. Twenty-four kilns, each to have a capacity of 50 cords, are in course of construction along the railway, and it is the intention to have the furnace ready for operation soon after the opening of navigation next spring, if possible. The ores will be brought by boat to the furnace from Marquette and Escunaba, and upon completion of the railroad, can be delivered by rail from Marquette. Mr. Horace E. Burt is general manager, with head-quarters on the ground.

On the Importance of giving Timely Attention to the Growth of Woodlands for the Supply of Charcoal for Metalurgical Uses.

[A paper read before the United States Association of Charcoal Iron Workers, in Harrisburg, Pennsylvania, October 21, 1880, by Franklin B. Hough, Chief of Forestry Division, United States Department of Agriculture.]

It will be conceded by every one interested in the use of charcoal that our woodlands, from which this essential material is derived, are being wasted, and used at a much more rapid rate than they are reproduced by natural growth, and that a time is approaching, and not distant, when the most careful attention must be given to the protection and care of our forests, if we would avoid the inconvenience from scarcity and high prices that must inevitably result from undue exhaustion of these supplies.

The penalties for improvidence will, doubtless, be sooner and more severely felt in the mining regions of our western States and Territories, where the scanty resources afforded in the cañons and secluded valleys of their mountains are already far spent, either from wasteful use or careless fires, and this in a region where restoration by re-planting is altogether beyond expectation or hope.

It is doubtless within the personal knowledge of every manufacturer using charcoal as a fuel that there are many places in the older settled States, in which forges and furnaces can no longer be worked with profit, because the woodlands that supplied the charcoal are all cleared away.

The same is true of many glass-works and other establishments, in which large quantities of wood are used as fuel. It is felt in every industry in which wood is used in any form as a material, either for fuel, for building purposes, or for manufacture; and this general tendency to exhaustion, without restoration, has now reached a point where it should arrest the attention of every thoughtful person, and lead to a serious consideration of the measures that can be taken for preventing the injuries that must inevitably result, unless timely precautions are adopted for preventing them.

In this matter, we may learn from the experience of older countries, in which a like tendency has been foreseen, and, to a large degree averted, by the adoption of measures tending to secure a careful regulation of the periods of cutting, and a systematic course of planting and management. But these regulations and restrictions imply an ownership of the soil, or, at least, authority in prescribing its course of management, which actually exists in these older and (so far as concern the forests) better governed countries than our own:—for in all of these countries where systems of forest administration are carried to greatest perfection, the Government itself owns large tracts of land, and there are extensive bodies of land belonging to local municipalities and to public institutions, over which the central government exercises its supervising protection and care.

In many of these woodlands, owned by communes and local municipalities, the inhabitants enjoy rights of usage and of common enjoyment, and these servitudes or common privileges, such as wood for fuel or for building, rights of pasturage or of gathering leaves and litter, &c., afford some of the most delicate and perplexing problems with which the Forest Administrations of these countries have to deal. Some of these rights originated so long ago that there appears to be no other authority than custom from time immemorial, and some of them are very liable to abuse. It is thus, for example, that excessive pasturage has exposed the mountains of France and Switzerland to the erosion of torrents, that it will cost millions of dollars to completely arrest, and restore to woodland protection, and it is from the removal of litter and dead leaves from the woods that the fertility of these lands has in other regions been seriously impaired. But in our own country we find quite a different state of affairs. Our National and our State governments own no forests that we can, at least at present, think of managing on a large scale at the public expense. Our counties, cities, and townships own no landed estates, and such of our public institutions as possess lands are managed by trustees, who would be quite as jealous of interference as are private owners.

By far the largest part, and in many of the States, the whole of the land, belongs to individuals, in absolute fee simple, and without any reservations or restrictions whatever, as regards the uses to which it may be applied. The owners may plant forests, or they may clear them away, without any interference from any quarter, provided always, that they do not injure their neighbors. Fortunately, there are no rights of common enjoyment known among us. The owner is absolute proprietor of the land and all the privileges belonging to it, except as here and there some mineral claim, or some hydraulic or other privilege may have been reserved in the sales made by former owners.

We therefore have, at the outset, a condition of affairs so entirely different from that which exists in Europe, that we cannot apply in practice any of the codes of regulation that there prevail. Their forest jurisprudence will afford us no precedents, and so far as detailed government are concerned, we can derive no aid from their experience.

But our general wants are the same as theirs, and so far as the methods of planting and management are concerned, we have much to learn from older countries; and every scientific principle that is determined, whether it involves a question in vegetable physiology, or in natural history, or in physics, becomes of common interest to all. Of the investigations and experiments that are being made at the various experimental stations in Europe, we should have early and accurate information as soon as published, and American investigators should do their full share in adding to the general fund of knowledge.

Returning from these general statements, to a particular consideration of the subject of present practical interest, let us notice some points that directly concern us:—the protection and restoration of woodlands devoted to the supply of charcoal. We have iron furnaces and other industries, of vital importance to our national welfare, depending upon supplies, that, like themselves, should be not only perpetual, but expanding, to meet the growing wants of a great nation, and the demands that new discoveries may require from year to year. These industries, and their supplies of every kind, are wholly independent of government control, and absolutely owned by individuals or corporations, upon whom alone depend their permanence and success. They can scarcely ask from the Government more than the legislation needed to maintain their rights, and that protection that is due to every citizen. The General or the State government may establish model plantations, and it may institute experiments to determine the best methods of management and the surest means for overcoming difficulties, but it cannot, at least for the present, undertake to supply the demand.

Whatever is done for the maintenance of our forest supplies must, therefore, be done by the owners of the soil, and it becomes a matter of present interest to consider how this can best be done, with a view of greatest profit, and for *permanent* success.

I emphasize the word "permanent," because I would wish to see measures adopted that should secure continued production, adequate to the continual wants of the country, due allowances being made for its growth, and due regard being had to the wants of those who are to come after us.

I need not stop to prove that a charcoal furnace, however well located, would, in due time, exhaust the woodlands around it, and that if these lands were turned over to agriculture as fast as they were cleared, the supplies would eventually cost more for transportation that the manufacturer could afford to pay. There must be an amount of woodland under the control or patronage of the furnace, sufficient to supply, by growth, the wood required for the charcoal that it uses, and we cannot count upon a durable supply, unless the management of these lands, during the intervals between cuttings, receives suitable care, so that they may deliver an adequate amount of material from year to year.

I am well aware that there is a wide difference between looking upon things *as they are* and *as they ought to be;* but, for the present, let us assume that a tract, or several tracts, of land suitable for the growth of wood, belong to the owners of the furnace, or are wholly subject to their orders at all times. The amount of land required for this object depends upon the quality of the soil, and of the underlying rock formations from which it has been decomposed; the nature of the sub-soil, its permeability to water, and its chemical components; the altitude, drainage, climate, kinds of timber, and other circumstances, so varied that no general rule can be stated. But whatever this amount may be, expressed in acres of woodland for the supply of one year, it is evident that there must be as many multiples of this in the whole tract, as there are years in the period between cuttings.

In scientific forestry, there are three general methods of cultivation employed, each of which has its own advantages, but only one of which could be profitably applied to the woodlands devoted to the growth of woods for charcoal. By the first of these, which the French call "*futaie*," and which, for lack of better term, we will call "high forest," a given tract of land is started as a forest, either by sowing or planting, and is regularly thinned out at stated periods, and kept free from useless undergrowth, until the timber is brought to full maturity, and is fit for the most important uses in civil and naval constructions. It is then removed, and a new crop is started, to grow on another century or more, for the uses of generations unborn. The profits, first and last, on this method of cultivation are very large, owing to the superior quality and quantity of the growth, and especially to the value of timber of large size, which increases, at an advanced period, in something like a geometrical ratio; and in a country where wood has a high price, the sale of thinnings, and of incidental profits, will sometimes pay the cost of management. But this cultivation for a long period, is better suited to the wants of a Goverment, for the supply of materials for its naval constructions, than to the demands of an industry that must have speedy returns for its investment; and the "*futaie*" affords no wood for charcoal, except in its thinnings and the tree tops.

By another mode of cultivation called by the French "*jardinage*," (literally "gardening,") trees are taken out here and there, from time to time, as they come to full maturity, or of a size proper for use. Such a forest presents a growth of all sizes and ages, at any one time, and, of course, the air and light come very unequally upon the trees at different stages of their growth. On examining the section of a tree thus grown, we would find the rings of growth more irregular than if all the trees had grown from one date, and the general quality as well as quantity would be inferior to that from the systematic cultivation first described. This rude and primitive system is the only one yet followed in the reserve wood-lots of our American farmers, where an attempt is made towards keeping up a supply of wood for local use, and it is the method followed in a wasteful way, in the timber leases of Canada, and the permits for lumbering in the forests of Maine, with this difference, that all the timber worth taking, is cut out at one operation, leaving the young trees to take care of themselves, till another thinning. Yet this method of "*jardinage*," slovenly as it may be, is the only one advisable in certain cases, as for example, where it would be dangerous to clear off the whole surface at once, lest drifting sands should get the mastery, or on steep declivities that might suffer from eroding torrents, or on the banks of rivers liable to inundation, where materials should always be at hand for making barriers.

I now come to the third principal method, known by the French as "*taillis*," corresponding nearly with our term "coppice," in which the whole of a woodland when cut off, is allowed to spring up in a new growth from the roots and stumps of the former growth. It is allowed to grow, with proper attention to protection and thinning, till the wood is suitable for firewood, or charcoal, and some pieces for use in manufactures, when the whole is again cut over and allowed to grow as before, the period varying from ten or fifteen to thirty or forty years. We have an instance of the shortest period in the osier willow, which is cut annually; a little longer one in the thickets, that are cut every four or five years for hoop poles; a little later for hop poles and vine props, and for stakes and poles for fences.

For the oak, that is peeled for tanning purposes, a period of about twenty or twenty-five years is allowed.

You will recognize in this, the mode of forest management that will most likely supply the charcoal of our future industries. Permit me to mention two requirements absolutely essential to its success: Protection against fires, and against domestic animals of every kind.

As to the first of these, it is evident that no amount of vigilance and precaution can be too great, and that in *prevention*, we must place our main reliance. It is among the rarest of events, that a forest fire is kindled by natural causes, such as lightning, or the friction between branches of trees, &c.

The former is usually accompanied by rain, and the other spontaneous causes are scarcely worth our time to consider. It is to man's agency, either from his carelessness or his misfortune, or his malevolence, that the origin of these fires may be traced, and it is of the highest importance that measures should be everywhere enforced in wooded countries, to prevent the disasters which happen from this cause. Perhaps the most common cause of these fires, is from the clearing of lands, the fires being set to burn off the brush and timber, and escaping beyond control. Fires from locomotives along the lines of railroads, are of daily occurrence in dry seasons, and often most disastrous in their consequences. The camp fires of hunters or fishermen, or of woodchoppers and lumbermen, the thoughtless fires set by idlers and children, the careless use of matches, the emptying of a pipe, or the throwing down of a lighted cigar, or the wad from a gun, may give origin to a fire that would annihilate the fortunes of a furnace, by burning over its whole tract of wood land, and every source of supply within its reach.

That such fires are sometimes set purposely, and with malicious intent, is probable, and against these, as other crimes, we have no remedy but adequate penalties rigorously enforced. But against careless or accidental fires we have no other safeguard than in preventive measures. And how shall these be secured? There is, perhaps, no more effectual means of making men careful, than by making them feel that they will, in some way, suffer for their negligence. The proprietor who hires men to cut a given quantity of wood, or to perform other work in a forest, has it in his power to prescribe rules in the use of camp fires, subject to the penalties of discharge for disobedience. The foreman of a job can be made to feel his responsibility for the men under his care, and can impress this upon every one under him. Locomotives can be run with safety, if specially arranged to prevent the falling of burning cinders, or the escape of burning sparks, as is done in those of best construction. It can be made a criminal offense to set fire to a fallow in clearing, without first notifying neighbors, and providing aid sufficient to control the fire that is set. The practice may be wholly forbidden by law, except in a season when there would be the least danger from the escape of fires. Persons who, from any cause, originate a fire, may be pecuniarily or personally punished, according to the degree of the damage or the fault of the offenders. Finally, there may be chosen annually, in each town, men specially authorized to take the direction of measures for arresting a forest fire, in case one gets once started and spreading, thus furnishing acknowledged leaders beforehand, and securing a methodical plan of operation when an emergency may arise. These wardens, by whatever name they may be known, should familiarize themselves with their districts, and with the roads and streams that might be made lines of defense. If regulations are established for the maintenance of plowed belts of land, or as to the time for burning fallows, it should be their duty to enforce their observance, and it should be their especial care to prosecute all offenders who might violate any of the laws or ordinances established for the prevention of damages, by the watchful care of fires.

Among the precautions against accident from fires, may be mentioned belts of freshly plowed land, more especially needed in prairie regions, but useful elsewhere, particularly on the borders of coniferous woodlands, which are more liable to suffer from fires than those of other kinds of timber. Cleared and cultivated belts of land along the sides of railroads and through woodlands are a useful precaution. The careful burning off of the inflammable materials from the surface, at a time when the fire spreads but slowly, and is entirely under control, is an excellent practice, especially along railroads.

Our legislation in reference to fires is very generally inadequate to the end proposed. We should have penalties for kindling a fire anywhere in the woods, without first clearing off all combustible material to a safe distance around it. It should be forbidden, under penalties, to leave such a fire burning, without attendance, whether any damages resulted, or not.

If we had a law that every man should pay full damages for

his carelessness, or, if unable, to pay these damages, that he should be imprisoned as a criminal, we should have greater vig ilance; and if railroad companies were required to pay for all the losses that result from fires set by their locomotives, we should hear less from the damages that they now occasion to our farms and woodlands.

The constant vigilance and precaution, that promise the best safeguards against forest fires, must, in a great degree, be the work of education, of precept, of admonition, and of penalties. We may hope that these will, in time, create a sentiment in the public mind that shall lead to an habitual caution, that will render these accidental fires unfrequent, and an administration of justice that shall pursue and punish the willful offender as surely as if the torch were applied to a building.

Before leaving this subject of forest fires, I will remark that their origin and means of prevention are, at the present time, a matter of special inquiry in connection with the Forestry investigations, under my charge, in the Department of Agriculture, at Washington, and I avail myself of this opportunity to invite every one who may have facts or suggestions, bearing upon the subject, to communicate them to me in writing. Blank forms of inquiry are sent to correspondents, with the view of collecting information, and the results, if sufficiently matured, will be included in the third Report upon Forestry, now in course of preparation.

As for protection against domestic animals, it is well known that no sprouts or undergrowth can live where they are allowed to range, and it is a most wasteful economy to sacrifice the hopes of a future wood-lot for the scanty pasturage that it affords. It is only when the growth is fairly above reach, and a woodland reserved for large timber, that cattle may be admitted without injury; but upon a tract designated for permanent wood growth, and in which there are always trees of small size, it is a safe rule to exclude them entirely, and at all seasons. The pasturage of sheep in hilly woodlands is more pernicious than that of cattle, because they root up the herbage, that gives coherence to the soil, and exposes it to the eroding action of rains and of torrents.

As regards the production from a given piece of woodland, as a general rule, a mixture of species will produce more material than one kind alone. The beech thrives, for example, very well with the oak, the former having a root that spreads near the surface, while the latter sends a strong tap-root deep into the subsoil.

A neglected woodland often tends to degenerate, the more valuable species being crowded out by those of more thrifty growth, but of poorer quality of wood. Void spaces may appear that should be filled by planting. Dead and decaying trees should be taken out, as well for use, while still of some worth, as to prevent the harboring of noxious insects, to the injury of the standing timber. Obstructions in streams, tending to their overflow, should be cleared out; swamps should be drained, which may sometimes be cheaply done by deepening their natural outlets, and dense thickets should be thinned out, so as to allow room for the more valuable kinds to grow.

No woodland can be called well kept, unless attention is given to the maintenance of roads for the removal of the products, and the quality and quantity of the timber can always be greatly improved by judicious management.

A tract designed for the permanent supply of a furnace, should be surveyed into as many sections of equal producing power, as there are years in the period of cutting, so that one of these may be cut over every year, taking in every case, all the trees large enough for use, but leaving the young sprouts for the new growth. In most species of deciduous trees, such as the oak, chestnut, ash, linden, &c., European foresters take care to cut them as near the ground as possible, and to dress off the stump with an adze, so that it shall be convex in form, to shed off the rain, and have a clean cut margin, around where the wood and the bark meet. Along this line, a row of buds will start, some of which will take independent root, and when thinned out, in due time, become trees. Sometimes the sprouts are bent down, partly cut, and covered with soil, so that they take root, and when able to grow alone, they are separated and become independent trees.

These are only a few of the many details that receive attention in older countries, where it has long since been found profitable to guide and direct a forest growth, assisting nature here and there as needed, and suppressing injurious influences from whatever source they appear—thereby securing a much greater amount of material in a given time, upon a tract of woodland, than can be realized if left to the chances of spontaneous growth.

It is a matter of regret, that such enormous waste is going on from year to year, in the use of our forest-products, which might, with proper care, be saved, and turned to profitable account. In lumbering operations, sometimes half of the trees represented in the tops and branches, and defective trunks are left to rot upon the ground, where they might be made into charcoal, or in some coniferous species, used in the manufacture of tar. In the peeling of hemlock trees for the bark, the entire body of the tree is often wasted, and in an extensive lumbering region that I lately visited, not one per cent. of the hemlock forests were turned to any account, after the bark was taken off. It is well worth inquiry, as to whether the slabs and other refuse of our great lumber mills might not be carbonized for metalurgical uses, instead of being burned to get rid of it, or being thrown into the streams to obstruct and polute their waters.

There are methods of carbonization devised with the special object of increasing the yield of charcoal, and saving the distilled products, that have a commercial value in the arts, and chips and saw-dust are now converted into illuminating gas, with great economy and success.

We have alluded to the wasteful peeling of our hemlock forests for tanning purposes. It does not need prophetic vision to foresee that an end of this practice will, sooner or later, come; for the hemlock tree is of slow growth, and seldom springs up as a second growth when it has once been cut away. Whenever this time may come, we shall be obliged to seek new materials for tanning, and there can be nothing more probable than that oak coppices will hereafter be grown in this country, for the supply of bark, as is done in many parts of Europe, the wood, after peeling, being used for charcoal or fire-wood. Would it not be worthy of our attention, therefore, in soils and locations where the kinds of oak best suited for tanning may be successfully grown, to give preference to this timber, for the double purpose of securing supplies of wood for charcoal and bark for tanning?

In the increasing scarcity of ash, hickory, and other woods used in manufactures, it must evidently become an object with the owners of woodlands to reserve from the cuttings, mainly intended for charcoal, such parts as have a greater value for cooperage, carriage-building, turning, and other manufactures, and, following the European custom, to reserve in their cuttings, here and there, the most promising specimens of the more valuable kinds, in order to give them ample opportunities for air and sunlight, till the next, or even the second, return of the period of cutting, when they will have acquired dimensions and value far greater than that required for charcoal.

Let us thoughtfully consider the profits from a growing tree:

If we examine its stump, we shall notice that is made up of concentric rings, each of which generally represents a year of growth. They are not all equal, for, in some seasons, the conditions have been more favorable, and, in other years, the tree may have lost its leaves prematurely from insect-ravages or a drouth, and the wood made that year is but slight. But for present illustration, let us regard the rings as of equal breadth, and, by a simple mathematical calculation, we have the following result:

Counting from the center outward, we have the series 1, 2, 3, 4, 5, &c. The sectional areas are as the squares of these numbers, or 1, 4, 9, 16, 25, &c., and the additional growth of each year is the difference of these successive squares, represented by the arithmetical series 3, 5, 7, 9, 11, 13, 15, &c., increasing outward by the common difference of 2.

It is evident from this that the growth of the third year is worth three times that of the second; that of the eighth year three times that of the fifth; and so on progressively, gaining in value at any given section, so long as the series is continued, and this, besides the gaining values from an increase in heighth. Is there any other rate of investment in which money pays such dividend as this? Can money be invested to better advantage, especially on broken and stony land, unsuited for agriculture, than in a thrifty well kept growth of woodland, which is gaining every year in value at these progressive rates?

There are many incidental benefits to agriculture and other interests that may be derived from the proper distribution of woodlands, and thère can be no doubt but that, if one fourth of the whole country were covered with forests properly distributed, the yield of cultivated fields would be as much or more than from the whole of the country under cultivation without them. The woodlands tend to mitigate the extremes of temperature and the force of winds. They promote humidity, and tend to prevent drouth. They retain the spring snows until they melt, and sink into the earth, and prevent drifting in winter. They maintain the flow of water in rivulets and streams, the water power of our brooks, and the supply of water needed for cities, and for the navigation of our rivers and canals. They afford nesting places for insectiverous birds, to the benefit of our fields and orchards; and lastly, but not least, they beautify and adorn the earth for man's health and happiness, to a degree we can best estimate, if we but imagine what a dreary waste the world would be without them.

As there is no class of industries so entirely dependent upon the woodlands for its success as that in which you are engaged, there is nothing more certain than that permanent success depends upon a maintenance of supplies, which can only be secured by a watchful care of the land when cut off, with the view of securing the best possible returns to woodland growth.

None are more directly interested than yourselves in diffusing, by precept and example, the idea that should be entertained by every owner of land, that there is profit, as well as beauty, in a growing tree.

I am well aware that in the scheme of management I have sketched—in which there is a specific task allotted to a given tract of land, in producing a certain amount of wood in a given time—I have described what *should be*, rather than what too often *does not exist*. There are many furnaces belonging to parties who do not own the woodlands that supply the charcoal which they use, and who, depending upon the present abundance around them, regard the present plenty as "inexhaustible," and take the chances of the future, without so much as a thought that it may fail them.

It is to such, especially, that these questions in Forestry more immediately relate, and they should not only realize themselves, but seek to diffuse the idea among others, that a rocky and rugged hill, a ravine, and often a plain, where, from long croping, without manuring, the surface soil has been exhausted, may be worth much more for woodland than for pasturage, or for any other use to which it can be applied, and that the time and money invested in its management will, in the end, yield a greater value for an inheritance, or for a market, than could possibly be realized from any other investment.

It may be a sordid motive to preach to mankind, that there is *money* to be made in an enterprise that involves so much that is grand and beautiful in nature; but alas! there are too many who will listen to no other. Let us avail ourselves of this incentive—and any other—if so be that it leads to the preservation and planting of woodlands, and be satisfied, without being inquisitive about the motive, provided that it leads to a good result. Above all, let us constantly remember, that this beautiful world, which owes half its beauty to sylvan scenery and woodland shade, is only held by us in trust for those who are to live after us, to use so far as may be needful, but not to desolate and destroy.

[It was impossible to get the discussion on this paper in time for the JOURNAL, and it is, therefore, deferred until the next issue.—ED.]

WE would invite the attention of members to our advertising space, and request their coöperation in securing advertisements, to assist in defraying expenses of JOURNAL. The next number will appear in January.

THE dues for the year 1881 are now being received. Our year commences October 1st. The dues are $10 for each iron-works, entitling it to two members and two copies of JOURNAL; additional members, each $5.

www.ingramcontent.com/pod-product-compliance
Lightning Source LLC
LaVergne TN
LVHW010603110826
845149LV00003B/749

* 9 7 8 1 4 1 8 1 8 7 4 5 3 *